FE

electrical
and computer
practice exam

Copyright © 2017 by NCEES®. All rights reserved.

All NCEES sample questions and solutions are copyrighted under the laws of the United States. No part of this publication may be reproduced, stored in a retrieval system, or transmitted in any form or by any means without the prior written permission of NCEES. Requests for permissions should be addressed in writing to permissions@ncees.org or to NCEES Exam Publications, PO Box 1686, Clemson, SC 29633.

ISBN 978-1-932613-82-7

Printed in the United States of America
1st printing March 2017

CONTENTS

Introduction to NCEES Exams 1
About NCEES
Exam Format
Examinee Guide
Scoring and reporting
Updates on exam content and procedures

Exam Specifications 3

Practice Exam 9

Solutions 81

About NCEES
NCEES is a nonprofit organization made up of the U.S. engineering and surveying licensing boards in all 50 states, U.S. territories, and the District of Columbia. We develop and score the exams used for engineering and surveying licensure in the United States. NCEES also promotes professional mobility through its services for licensees and its member boards.

Engineering licensure in the United States is regulated by licensing boards in each state and territory. These boards set and maintain the standards that protect the public they serve. As a result, licensing requirements and procedures vary by jurisdiction, so stay in touch with your board (ncees.org/licensing-boards).

Exam Format
The FE exam contains 110 questions and is administered year-round via computer at approved Pearson VUE test centers. A 6-hour appointment time includes a tutorial, the exam, and a break. You'll have 5 hours and 20 minutes to complete the actual exam.

Beginning July 1, 2017, in addition to traditional multiple-choice questions with one correct answer, the FE exam will use common alternative item types such as

- Multiple correct options—allows multiple choices to be correct
- Point and click—requires examinees to click on part of a graphic to answer
- Drag and drop—requires examinees to click on and drag items to match, sort, rank, or label
- Fill in the blank—provides a space for examinees to enter a response to the question

To familiarize yourself with the format, style, and navigation of a computer-based exam, view the demo on ncees.org/ExamPrep.

Examinee Guide
The *NCEES Examinee Guide* is the official guide to policies and procedures for all NCEES exams. During exam registration and again on exam day, examinees must agree to abide by the conditions in the *Examinee Guide*, which includes the CBT Examinee Rules and Agreement. You can download the *Examinee Guide* at ncees.org/exams. It is your responsibility to make sure you have the current version.

Scoring and reporting
Exam results for computer-based exams are typically available 7–10 days after you take the exam. You will receive an email notification from NCEES with instructions to view your results in your MyNCEES account. All results are reported as pass or fail.

Updates on exam content and procedures
Visit us at **ncees.org/exams** for updates on everything exam-related, including specifications, exam-day policies, scoring, and corrections to published exam preparation materials. This is also where you will register for the exam and find additional steps you should follow in your state to be approved for the exam.

EXAM SPECIFICATIONS

Fundamentals of Engineering (FE)
ELECTRICAL AND COMPUTER CBT Exam Specifications
Effective Beginning with the January 2014 Examinations

- The FE exam is a computer-based test (CBT). It is closed book with an electronic reference.

- Examinees have 6 hours to complete the exam, which contains 110 multiple-choice questions. The 6-hour time also includes a tutorial and an optional scheduled break.

- The FE exam uses both the International System of Units (SI) and the U.S. Customary System (USCS).

Knowledge	Number of Questions
1. Mathematics A. Algebra and trigonometry B. Complex numbers C. Discrete mathematics D. Analytic geometry E. Calculus F. Differential equations G. Linear algebra H. Vector analysis	11–17
2. Probability and Statistics A. Measures of central tendencies and dispersions (e.g., mean, mode, standard deviation) B. Probability distributions (e.g., discrete, continuous, normal, binomial) C. Expected value (weighted average) in decision making D. Estimation for a single mean (e.g., point, confidence intervals, conditional probability)	4–6
3. Ethics and Professional Practice A. Codes of ethics (professional and technical societies) B. NCEES *Model Law* and *Model Rules* C. Intellectual property (e.g., copyright, trade secrets, patents)	3–5
4. Engineering Economics A. Time value of money (e.g., present value, future value, annuities) B. Cost estimation C. Risk identification D. Analysis (e.g., cost-benefit, trade-off, breakeven)	3–5

5. **Properties of Electrical Materials**   4–6
   A. Chemical (e.g., corrosion, ions, diffusion)
   B. Electrical (e.g., conductivity, resistivity, permittivity, magnetic permeability)
   C. Mechanical (e.g., piezoelectric, strength)
   D. Thermal (e.g., conductivity, expansion)

6. **Engineering Sciences**   6–9
   A. Work, energy, power, heat
   B. Charge, energy, current, voltage, power
   C. Forces (e.g., between charges, on conductors)
   D. Work done in moving a charge in an electric field (relationship between voltage and work)
   E. Capacitance
   F. Inductance

7. **Circuit Analysis (DC and AC Steady State)**   10–15
   A. KCL, KVL
   B. Series/parallel equivalent circuits
   C. Thevenin and Norton theorems
   D. Node and loop analysis
   E. Waveform analysis (e.g., RMS, average, frequency, phase, wavelength)
   F. Phasors
   G. Impedance

8. **Linear Systems**   5–8
   A. Frequency/transient response
   B. Resonance
   C. Laplace transforms
   D. Transfer functions
   E. 2-port theory

9. **Signal Processing**   5–8
   A. Convolution (continuous and discrete)
   B. Difference equations
   C. Z-transforms
   D. Sampling (e.g., aliasing, Nyquist theorem)
   E. Analog filters
   F. Digital filters

10. **Electronics** 7–11
    A. Solid-state fundamentals (e.g., tunneling, diffusion/drift current, energy bands, doping bands, p-n theory)
    B. Discrete devices (diodes, transistors, BJT, CMOS) and models and their performance
    C. Bias circuits
    D. Amplifiers (e.g., single-stage/common emitter, differential)
    E. Operational amplifiers (ideal, non-ideal)
    F. Instrumentation (e.g., measurements, data acquisition, transducers)
    G. Power electronics

11. **Power** 8–12
    A. Single phase and three phase
    B. Transmission and distribution
    C. Voltage regulation
    D. Transformers
    E. Motors and generators
    F. Power factor (pf)

12. **Electromagnetics** 5–8
    A. Maxwell equations
    B. Electrostatics/magnetostatics (e.g., measurement of spatial relationships, vector analysis)
    C. Wave propagation
    D. Transmission lines (high frequency)
    E. Electromagnetic compatibility

13. **Control Systems** 6–9
    A. Block diagrams (feed-forward, feedback)
    B. Bode plots
    C. Closed-loop and open-loop response
    D. Controller performance (gain, PID), steady-state errors
    E. Root locus
    F. Stability
    G. State variables

14. **Communications** 5–8
    A. Basic modulation/demodulation concepts (e.g., AM, FM, PCM)
    B. Fourier transforms/Fourier series
    C. Multiplexing (e.g., time division, frequency division)
    D. Digital communications

15. **Computer Networks** 3–5
    A. Routing and switching
    B. Network topologies/frameworks/models
    C. Local area networks

16. **Digital Systems** 7–11
    A. Number systems
    B. Boolean logic
    C. Logic gates and circuits
    D. Logic minimization (e.g., SOP, POS, Karnaugh maps)
    E. Flip-flops and counters
    F. Programmable logic devices and gate arrays
    G. State machine design
    H. Data path/controller design
    I. Timing (diagrams, asynchronous inputs, races, hazards)

17. **Computer Systems** 4–6
    A. Architecture (e.g., pipelining, cache memory)
    B. Microprocessors
    C. Memory technology and systems
    D. Interfacing

18. **Software Development** 4–6
    A. Algorithms
    B. Data structures
    C. Software design methods (structured, object-oriented)
    D. Software implementation (e.g., procedural, scripting languages)
    E. Software testing

ID: 8
PRACTICE EXAM

FE ELECTRICAL AND COMPUTER PRACTICE EXAM

1. Given the following triangle, the length (cm) of Side AB is most nearly:

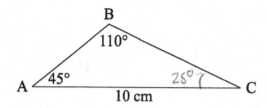

- A. 4.5
- B. 7.1
- C. 7.5
- D. 192

2. The term $\dfrac{(1-i)^2}{(1+i)^2}$, where $i = \sqrt{-1}$ is most nearly:

- A. $1 + i$
- B. 0
- C. $-1 + i$
- D. -1

FE ELECTRICAL AND COMPUTER PRACTICE EXAM

3. Two complex numbers A and B are as follows:

    $A = 10 + j3$
    $B = -6 + j4$

    The quotient A/B is most nearly:

    - A. $-0.92 + j1.12$
    - B. $0.92 - j1.12$
    - ● C. $-0.92 - j1.12$
    - D. $0.92 + j1.12$

4. Three lines are defined by the three equations:

    $x + y = 0$
    $x - y = 0$
    $2x + y = 1$

    The three lines form a triangle with vertices at:

    - ● A. $(0, 0), \left(\dfrac{1}{3}, \dfrac{1}{3}\right), (1, -1)$
    - B. $(0, 0), \left(\dfrac{2}{3}, \dfrac{2}{3}\right), (-1, -1)$
    - C. $(1, 1), (1, -1), (2, 1)$
    - D. $(1, 1), (3, -3), (-2, -1)$

FE ELECTRICAL AND COMPUTER PRACTICE EXAM

5. The only point of inflection on the curve representing the equation $y = x^3 + x^2 - 3$ is at:

- A. $x = -\dfrac{2}{3}$
- B. $x = -\dfrac{1}{3}$
- C. $x = 0$
- D. $x = \dfrac{1}{3}$

6. Given the function $f(x, y) = x^2 + xy + y^2$, solve for $\dfrac{\partial f}{\partial y}$.

- A. $2x + x + y + 2y$
- B. $2x + y$
- C. $2y$
- D. $x + 2y$ ●

7. The following equation describes a second-order system:

$$\frac{d^2y}{dt^2} + 6\frac{dy}{dt} + 25y = x(t)$$

The system may be described as:

- A. nonlinear ●
- B. overdamped
- C. critically damped
- D. underdamped

8. The general solution to $y'' + 4y' + 4y = 0$ is:

   - A. $C_1 e^{-4x}$
   - B. $C_1 e^{-2x}$
   - C. $e^{-4x}(C_1 + C_2 x)$
   - D. $e^{-2x}(C_1 + C_2 x)$

9. The magnitude of the resultant of the three coplanar vectors, A, B, and C, is most nearly:

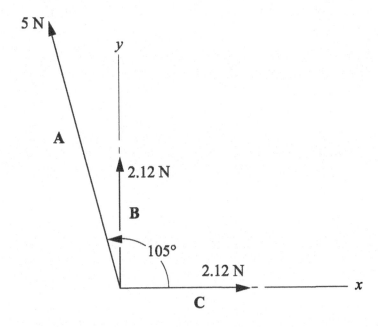

   - A. 7.0
   - B. 7.8
   - C. 9.2
   - D. 10.3

FE ELECTRICAL AND COMPUTER PRACTICE EXAM

10. Which of the following is a unit vector perpendicular to the plane determined by the vectors **A** = 2**i** + 4**j** and **B** = **i** + **j** − **k**?

    - A. −2**i** + **j** − **k**
    - B. $\frac{1}{\sqrt{5}}(\mathbf{i} + 2\mathbf{j})$
    - C. $\frac{1}{\sqrt{6}}(-2\mathbf{i} + \mathbf{j} - \mathbf{k})$
    - D. $\frac{1}{\sqrt{6}}(-2\mathbf{i} - \mathbf{j} - \mathbf{k})$

11. For a series of measurements resulting in values of 11, 11, 11, 11, 12, 13, 13, 14, the arithmetic mean is 12. The median value is:

    - A. 12.5
    - B. 12.0
    - C. 11.5
    - D. 11.0

12. The test scores for a class followed a normal distribution. The distribution of the scores follows the density function shown below. The mean score for the class is found to be 78, with a standard deviation of 8.5. Where would you expect a score of 90 to appear on the graph?

Mark the correct region of the graph.

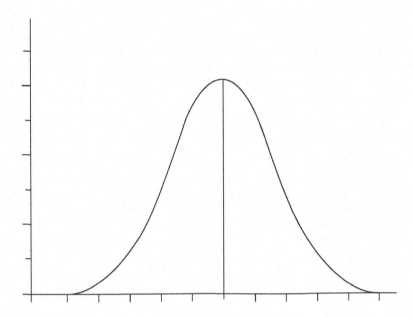

FE ELECTRICAL AND COMPUTER PRACTICE EXAM

13. Suppose the lengths of telephone calls form a normal distribution with a mean length of 8.0 min and a standard deviation of 2.5 min. The probability that a telephone call selected at random will last more than 15.5 min is most nearly:

    - A. 0.0013
    - B. 0.0026
    - C. 0.2600
    - D. 0.9987

14. You have a fair coin that you toss ten times. The probability of getting exactly four heads in ten tosses is most nearly:

    - A. 0.1
    - B. 0.2
    - C. 0.4
    - D. 0.5

FE ELECTRICAL AND COMPUTER PRACTICE EXAM

15. You are a student and have an on-site job interview with Company A. Just before you fly to the interview, you get a call from Company B asking you to come for an on-site interview at their offices in the same city. When you inform them of your interview with Company A, they suggest you stop in after that. Company A has already paid for your airfare and, at the conclusion of your interview with them, issues you reimbursement forms for the balance of your trip expenses with instructions to file for all of your trip expenses. When you inform them of your added interview stop at Company B, they tell you to go ahead and charge the entire cost of the trip to Company A. You interview with Company B, and at the conclusion, they give you travel reimbursement forms with instructions to file for all of your trip expenses. When you inform them of the instructions of Company A, they tell you that the only expenses requiring receipts are airfare and hotel rooms, so you should still file for all the other expenses with them even if Company A is paying for it because students always need a little spending money. What should you do?

- A. File for travel expenses with only one firm.
- B. Do as both recruiting officers told you. It is their money and their travel policies.
- C. Try to divide the expenses between both firms as best you can.
- D. Tell all of your classmates to sign up to interview with these firms for the trips.

16. An engineer testifying as an expert witness in a product liability case should:

- A. avoid answering questions from the opposing attorney
- B. provide a complete and objective analysis within his or her area of competence
- C. provide an evaluation of the character of the defendant
- D. provide information on the professional background of the defendant

FE ELECTRICAL AND COMPUTER PRACTICE EXAM

17. An engineer judges that a design poses a threat to human life and recommends to management that the design must be modified. The manager, who is not an engineer, overrules the recommendation. According to the *Model Rules*, the engineer must:

    - A. resign from the job
    - B. inform the employer, and any other appropriate authority, of the problem
    - C. contact the press and make it clear that this is a professional opinion
    - D. comply with the manager's ruling

18. According to the *Model Rules*, Section 240.15, Rules of Professional Conduct, licensed professional engineers are obligated to:

    - A. ensure that design documents and surveys are reviewed by a panel of licensed engineers prior to affixing a seal of approval
    - B. express public opinions under the direction of an employer or client regardless of knowledge of subject matter
    - C. practice by performing services only in the areas of their competence and in accordance with the current standards of technical competence
    - D. offer, give, or solicit services directly or indirectly in order to secure work or other valuable or political considerations

19. The annual nominal interest rate on the unpaid portion of a contract is 17%. If the interest is compounded quarterly, the effective interest rate is most nearly:

- A. 14%
- B. 16%
- C. 18%
- D. 20%

20. A printer costs $900. Its salvage value after 5 years is $300. Annual maintenance is $50. If the interest rate is 8%, the equivalent uniform annual cost is most nearly:

- A. $224
- B. $300
- C. $327
- D. $350

FE ELECTRICAL AND COMPUTER PRACTICE EXAM

21. A project has the estimated cash flows shown below.

Year End	0	1	2	3	4
Cash Flow	−$1,100	−$400	+$1,000	+$1,000	+$1,000

Using an interest rate of 12% per year compounded annually, the annual worth of the project is most nearly:

- A. $450
- B. $361
- C. $320
- D. $226

22. Which of the following situations is most appropriate for using break-even analysis?

- A. Calculating the interest rate that will ensure that costs and returns are equal
- B. Determining the number of units to produce to ensure that income covers expenses
- C. Establishing the minimum return on an investment over a set number of years
- D. Forecasting the amount of product that must be produced to meet a set profit margin

23. Which of the following occurs in the reaction $Cu^{2+} + Zn \rightarrow Cu + Zn^{2+}$?

- A. Only copper is oxidized.
- B. Only zinc is oxidized.
- C. Both copper and zinc are oxidized.
- D. Neither copper nor zinc is oxidized.

24. A corrosion protection system is to be designed to protect a cast iron pipe. Which one of the following metals would be able to serve as a sacrificial anode (corrodes before the pipe)?

- A. Pb
- B. Ni
- C. Cu
- D. Zn

25. If an aluminum crimp connector were used to connect a copper wire to a battery, what would you expect to happen?

- A. Only the copper wire will corrode.
- B. Only the aluminum connector will corrode.
- C. Both will corrode.
- D. Nothing

26. The solid cylindrical conductor shown below carries a uniform direct current having a density of 100 A/m² in the positive z direction. Assume the resistivity is 0.1 Ω·m.

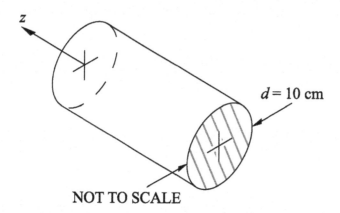

NOT TO SCALE

The power loss (W) per meter length is most nearly:

- A. 2.50
- B. 3.93
- C. 7.85
- D. 31.42

27. The power (W) dissipated in the 90-Ω resistor of the circuit shown below is most nearly:

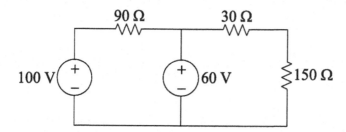

- A. 8
- B. 18
- C. 40
- D. 71

28. A 10-µF capacitor has been charged to a potential of 150 V. A resistor of 25 Ω is then connected across the capacitor through a switch. When the switch is closed for ten time constants, the total energy (joules) dissipated by the resistor is most nearly:

- A. 1.0×10^{-7}
- B. 1.1×10^{-1}
- C. 9.0×10^{1}
- D. 9.0×10^{3}

29. Two point charges of 5 C and –12 C are separated in air by a distance of 30 cm. The permittivity of air is 8.85×10^{-12} F/m. Assume that dielectric breakdown does not occur. The force of repulsion (N) between the spheres is most nearly:

- A. -7.4×10^{12}
- B. -6×10^{12}
- C. -6×10^{10}
- D. 6×10^{16}

FE ELECTRICAL AND COMPUTER PRACTICE EXAM

30. An electron with mass (9.1×10^{-31} kg) is released from the cathode in a vacuum and accelerates toward the anode, which is 0.1 m away and is at +20,000 V with respect to the cathode. When the electron reaches the anode, its velocity (m/s) is most nearly:

- A. 59×10^6
- B. 83×10^6
- C. 265×10^6
- D. 35×10^{24}

31. Point A has coordinates of $x = 5$ m, $y = 0$ m, $z = 1$ m. Point B has coordinates of $x = 0$ m, $y = 0$ m, and $z = 4$ m. Given an electric field of $\bar{E} = 2\bar{a}_x + 3\bar{a}_y + 4\bar{a}_z$ V/m, the amount of energy (J) required to move a 3.25 µC point charge from Point A to Point B is most nearly:

- A. -2
- B. -6.5×10^{-6}
- C. 22.8×10^{-6}
- D. 2

FE ELECTRICAL AND COMPUTER PRACTICE EXAM

32. After having been closed for a long time, the switch is opened at $t = 0$.

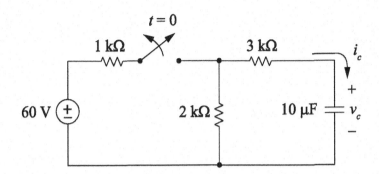

The energy (mJ) dissipated in the 2-kΩ resistor for the period $t = 0^+$ to $t = \infty$ is most nearly:

- A. 1.6
- B. 3.2
- C. 6.0
- D. 8.0

33. In the circuit shown, voltage V_O (V) is most nearly:

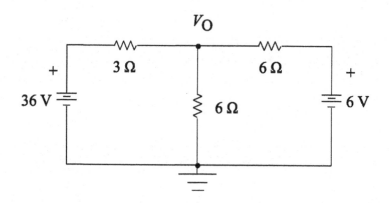

- A. 19.5
- B. 18.5
- C. 16.5
- D. 3.0

34. The current (amperes) through the 6-Ω resistor is most nearly:

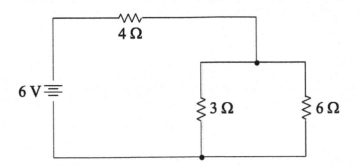

- A. 1/3
- B. 1/2
- C. 1
- D. 3/2

35. In the resistor circuit shown below, the equivalent resistance R_{eq} (Ω) at Terminals a-b is most nearly:

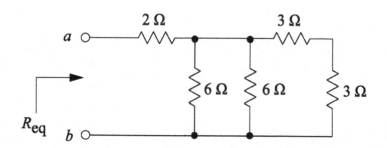

- A. 22
- B. 20
- C. 4
- D. 2

36. Refer to the figure below.

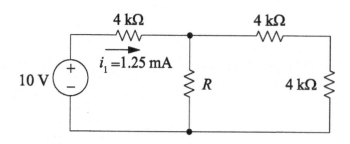

The value (kΩ) of R needed to make i_1 equal 1.25 mA is most nearly _____.

Answer to the nearest integer.

FE ELECTRICAL AND COMPUTER PRACTICE EXAM

37. The circuit shown in Figure 1 is presented as the Norton equivalent circuit in Figure 2. The value of R_N (Ω) is most nearly:

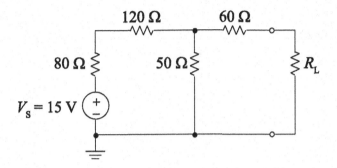

FIGURE 1

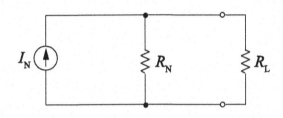

FIGURE 2

- A. 50
- B. 60
- C. 100
- D. 120

38. Consider the following circuit:

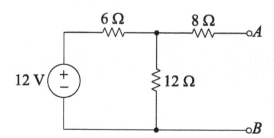

The Thevenin equivalent resistance (Ω) at Points A–B is most nearly:

- A. 8
- B. 12
- C. 20
- D. 26

39. Two waveforms are represented by the following equations:

$i_1 = 10 \cos(\omega t) - 7 \cos(3\omega t) - 3 \sin(5\omega t)$
$i_2 = 10 \sin(\omega t) + 3 \cos(3\omega t) + 7 \cos(5\omega t)$

How do their RMS values compare?

- A. RMS values of $i_1(t)$ and $i_2(t)$ are non-zero and equal.
- B. RMS value of $i_1(t)$ is larger than that of $i_2(t)$.
- C. RMS value of $i_1(t)$ is smaller than that of $i_2(t)$.
- D. RMS values of $i_1(t)$ and $i_2(t)$ are each zero.

40. Consider the following circuit in the time domain:

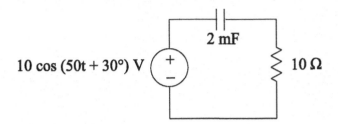

Label the circuit below with component values that yield the equivalent circuit in the frequency (phasor) domain.

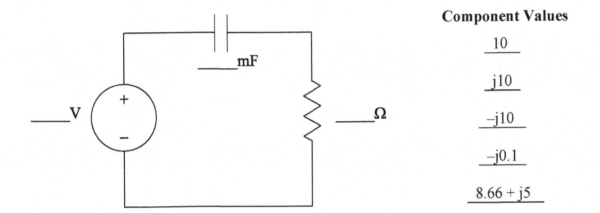

Component Values

10

j10

–j10

–j0.1

8.66 + j5

41. A 1,000-Ω resistor is in series with a 2-mH inductor. An ac-voltage source operating at a frequency of 100,000 rad/s is attached as shown in the figure. The impedance (Ω) of the *RL* combination is most nearly:

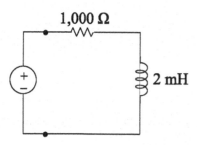

- A. $200 + j\,1{,}000$
- B. $1{,}000 + j\,200$
- C. $38.4 + j\,192$
- D. $1{,}000 - j\,200$

42. Series-connected circuit elements are shown in the figure below.

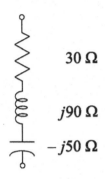

Which of the following impedance diagrams is correct according to conventional notation?

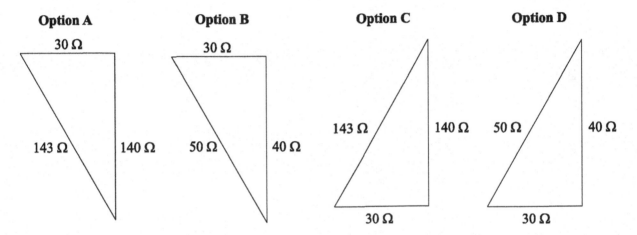

- A. Option A
- B. Option B
- C. Option C
- D. Option D

43. After having been closed for a long time, the switch shown in the figure is opened at $t = 0$.

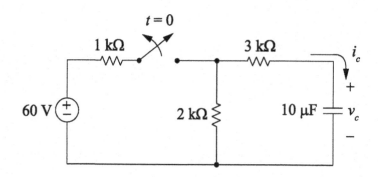

The expression for v_c (V) for $t > 0$ is most nearly:

- A. $20\, e^{-50t}$
- B. $20\, e^{-0.2t}$
- C. $40\, e^{-200,000t}$
- D. $40\, e^{-20t}$

44. In the circuit shown below, the frequency of the voltage source can be varied over a broad range of frequencies while the amplitude of the input voltage is kept constant. The frequency (kHz) at which v_o has maximum amplitude is most nearly:

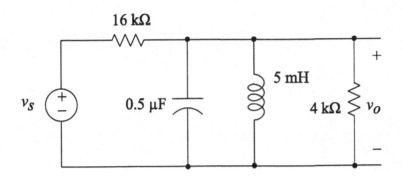

- A. 1.59
- B. 3.18
- C. 15.9
- D. 31.8

45. Consider the following network:

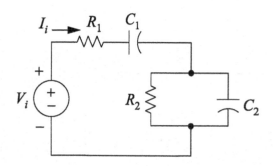

The driving point impedance (input impedance) has poles at:

- A. $s = 0$ and $s = -\dfrac{1}{R_2 C_2}$

- B. $s = -\dfrac{1}{R_1 C_1}$ and $s = -\dfrac{1}{R_2 C_2}$

- C. $s = 0$ and $s = -\dfrac{1}{R_1 C_2}$

- D. $s = -\dfrac{1}{R_1 C_2}$ and $s = -\dfrac{1}{R_2 C_1}$

46. The circuit shown below has a transfer function given by $V_{out}/V_{in} = \dfrac{1.2(s+2)}{(s+1)(s+4)}$. V_{in} is a unit step function, and there is no initial charge on the capacitors. The final (steady-state) value of $V_{out}(t)$ (V) is most nearly:

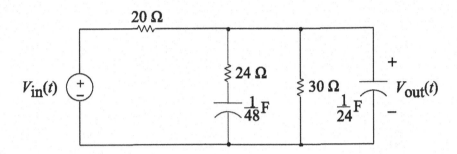

- A. 0
- B. 0.04
- C. 0.55
- D. 0.60

47. The function $x(t)$ shown below is to be convolved with $h(t)$, also shown below.

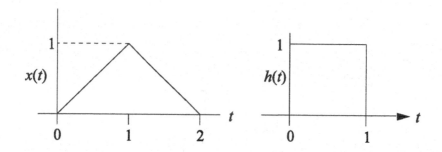

If $y(t)$ is the value of the convolution $x(t) * h(t)$, for $1 < t < 2$, the value of $y(t)$ is most nearly:

47. (Continued)

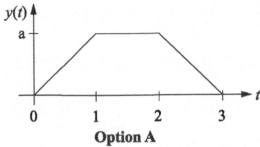
Option A

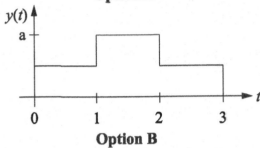
Option B

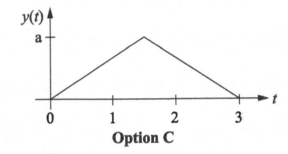
Option C

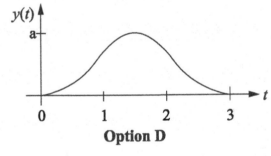
Option D

- A. Option A
- B. Option B
- C. Option C
- D. Option D

48. The function $x(t)$ is to be convolved with $h(t)$. Both functions are shown below.

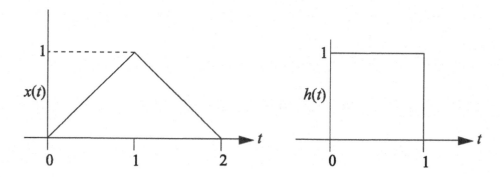

The value of the convolution of $x(t)$ with $h(t)$ for $0 \leq t \leq 1$ is most nearly:

- A. $t/2$
- B. t
- C. $t^2/2$
- D. t^2

49. A digital filter with input $x[k]$ and output $y[k]$ is described by the difference equation:

$$y[k] = \frac{1}{6}(3x[k] + 2x[k-1] + x[k-2])$$

The discrete-time transfer function of the filter $H(z)$ is:

- A. $\dfrac{6z^2}{3z^2 + 2z + 1}$
- B. $\dfrac{6z}{3z^2 + 2z + 1}$
- C. $3z^2 + 2z + 1$
- D. $\dfrac{1}{6}\left[\dfrac{3z^2 + 2z + 1}{z^2}\right]$

FE ELECTRICAL AND COMPUTER PRACTICE EXAM

50. The sifting property of the impulse (delta) function $\delta(t)$ is defined as

$$\int_{-\infty}^{\infty} f(t)\delta(t-a)dt = f(a)$$

The value of the integral

$$\int_{-\infty}^{\infty} \cos(\omega t)\delta(t-1)dt \text{ where } \omega = 2$$

radians per second and t is in seconds is most nearly:

- A. −0.4161
- B. 0
- C. 0.9093
- D. 1.0

51. For a *pn* junction, the contact potential V_0 is:

- A. a measure of the ohmic resistance of the junction
- B. a built-in potential barrier that is necessary for equilibrium at the junction
- C. independent of charge carrier concentrations in the *p* and *n* regions
- D. independent of temperature

52. The thermal voltage for a silicon P-N junction kept at a temperature of 0°C is most nearly:

- A. 26 V
- B. 23.5 V
- C. 26 mV
- D. 23.5 mV

53. The gate-to-source voltage of the depletion-mode, n-channel MOSFET shown below is 1 V. The various operating regions of the MOSFET are described below:

Cutoff Region: ($v_{GS} < V_p$)
 $i_D = 0$
Triode Region: ($v_{GS} > V_p$ and $v_{GD} > V_p$)
 $i_D = K[2(v_{GS} - V_p)v_{DS} - v_{DS}^2]$
Saturation Region: ($v_{GS} > V_p$ and $v_{GD} < V_p$)
 $i_D = K(v_{GS} - V_p)^2$

If $K = 0.2$ mA/V² and $V_p = -4$ V, the value of i_D (mA) is most nearly:

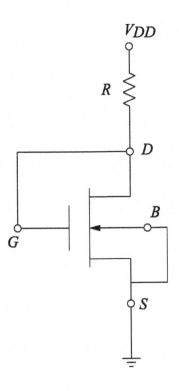

- A. 5
- B. 2.2
- C. 1.8
- D. 0

54. An n-channel JFET has a pinch-off voltage V_p of –4 V and I_{DSS} of 16 mA. This device is to operate in the saturation region. When the quiescent drain current is 4 mA, the gate-to-source voltage (V) required to give this operating point is most nearly:

- A. –2.0
- B. –2.5
- C. –3.0
- D. –4.0

55. Let R_c = 600 Ω, and let R_E = 500 Ω. When R_1 = 2.00 kΩ and R_2 = 1.00 kΩ, the value of I_C (mA) is most nearly:

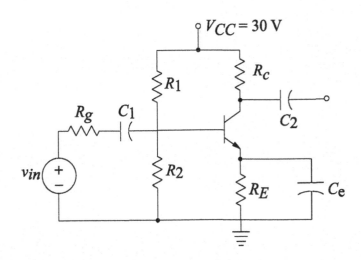

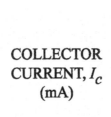

R_g = 100 Ω
C_1 = 10.0 µF
C_2 = 10.0 µF
C_e = 50.0 µF
V_{BE} = 0.7 V

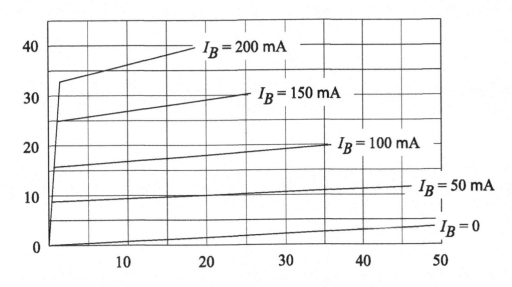

- ○ A. 10
- ○ B. 19
- ○ C. 24
- ○ D. 27

56. The transistor in the circuit below has a very high value of β.

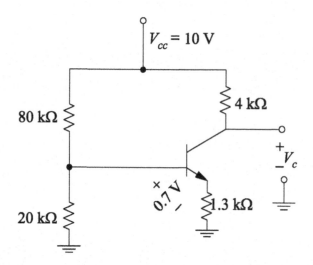

The value of the collector voltage V_c (V) is most nearly:

- A. 6.0
- B. 4.0
- C. 2.0
- D. 1.3

57. The figure shows an ideal operational amplifier circuit. The voltage gain of the circuit V_{out}/V_{in} is most nearly:

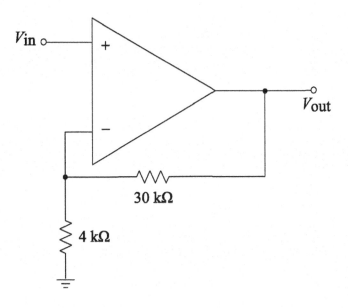

- ○ A. 8.5
- ○ B. 7.5
- ○ C. 5.0
- ○ D. 4.0

58. An ideal operational amplifier is to be connected as a differential amplifier as shown in the diagram below. Nominally, $R_1 = R_3 = 5$ kΩ and $R_2 = R_4 = 200$ kΩ.

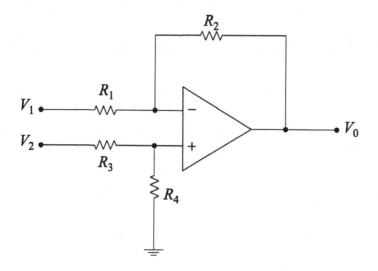

The gain for an input V_2 with the input V_1 grounded is most nearly:

- A. 20
- B. 35
- C. 40
- D. 41

59. A balanced 3-phase source can be represented by three wye-connected generators, as shown below.

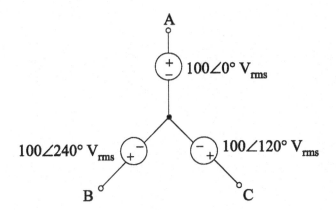

The line-to-line voltage V_{AB} (V_{rms}) is most nearly:

- A. 173.2∠30°
- B. 173.2∠−30°
- C. 57.7∠30°
- D. 57.7∠−30°

FE ELECTRICAL AND COMPUTER PRACTICE EXAM

60. A 3-phase induction motor is operating at a speed of $n = 3{,}500$ rpm with a line voltage of 240 V at 60 Hz. The number of poles this motor has is most nearly:

- A. 2
- B. 4
- C. 6
- D. 8

61. A single-phase induction motor is rated at 440 V_{rms}, 10 hp, 85% efficiency, and 0.6 pf lagging. The magnitude (amperes) of the rms motor current is most nearly:

- A. 33.2
- B. 28.3
- C. 19.9
- D. 16.9

62. A 3-phase induction motor is operating at a speed of $n = 3{,}500$ rpm with a line voltage of 240 V at 60 Hz. The number of poles this motor has is most nearly:

- A. 2
- B. 4
- C. 5.83
- D. 6

FE ELECTRICAL AND COMPUTER PRACTICE EXAM

63. A pump station uses an induction motor that requires a complex power of:

$S_1 = 20 \angle 36.87°$ kVA

and a synchronous motor that requires a complex power of:

$S_2 = 10 \angle -53.13°$ kVA.

The reactive power (kVAR) required by the pump station is most nearly:

- A. 4
- B. 20
- C. 22
- D. 30

64. An ammeter, a voltmeter, and a wattmeter were installed in an AC circuit and read 15 A_{rms}, 115 V_{rms}, and 1,500 W, respectively. The power factor of the circuit is most nearly:

- A. 0.5
- B. 0.7
- C. 0.87
- D. 1.0

65. A balanced 3-phase load is rated at 100 kVA and 0.65 pf lagging. A purely capacitive load is added in parallel with the inductive load to improve the power factor to 0.9 lagging. The capacitive load must supply a reactive power (kVAR) that is most nearly:

- A. 76
- B. 65
- C. 45
- D. 31

66. If the complex power is 1,500 VA with a power factor of 0.866 lagging, the reactive power (VAR) is most nearly:

- A. 0
- B. 750
- C. 1,300
- D. 1,500

FE ELECTRICAL AND COMPUTER PRACTICE EXAM

67. One tesla represents a very strong magnetic flux density. The current (amperes) required in a long straight wire to produce a 1-tesla flux density at 0.5 m from the wire in free space (use $\mu = \mu_0$) is most nearly:

- A. 1.25×10^6
- B. 2.5×10^6
- C. 5×10^6
- D. 25×10^6

68. A coaxial cable transmission line is known to have a characteristic impedance of 50 Ω. Measurement of the capacitance between the center conductor and the outer shield indicates a capacitance per unit length of 133 pF/m. The inductance per unit length of the coaxial cable is most nearly:

- A. 6.6 nH/m
- B. 33 nH/m
- C. 0.33 μH/m
- D. 3.3 μH/m

69. The following circuit contains a lossless transmission line with a characteristic impedance of $Z_0 = 50\ \Omega$. The magnitude of the load voltage V_L is 200 V_{rms}.

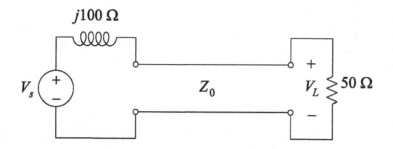

The magnitude of the source voltage V_S (V_{rms}) is most nearly:

- A. 100.0
- B. 200.0
- C. 282.8
- D. 447.2

70. A lossless high-frequency transmission line has a characteristic impedance $Z_0 = 50\ \Omega$ and an inductance per unit length of 5 mH/m. The capacitance per unit length (μF/m) is most nearly:

- A. 1
- B. 2
- C. 5
- D. 10

71. The asymptotic Bode plot for the magnitude of the transfer function $T(s)$ is shown in the figure below. The transfer function $T(s)$ in terms of the asymptotic Bode plot is most nearly:

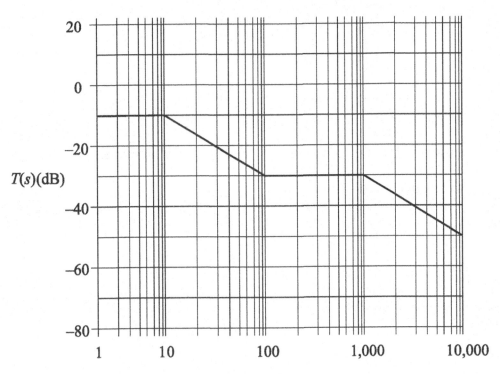

ASYMPTOTIC BODE PLOT

- A. $T(s) = K \dfrac{(s+100)}{(s+10)(s+1,000)}$
- B. $T(s) = K \dfrac{(s+100)}{s(s+10)(s+1,000)}$
- C. $T(s) = K \dfrac{s(s+100)}{(s+10)(s+1,000)}$
- D. $T(s) = K \dfrac{(s+10)(s+1,000)}{(s+1)(s+100)}$

72. A proportional controller with gain K is used to control a spring and mass system as shown in the figure below.

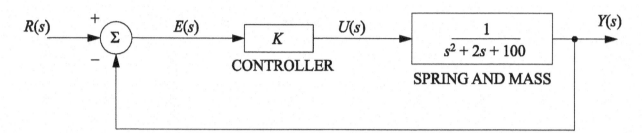

If K is adjusted so that the second-order closed-loop system model is $\dfrac{Y(s)}{R(s)} = \dfrac{50}{s^2 + 2s + 150}$, then the system damping ratio is most nearly:

- A. 0.8
- B. 0.08
- C. 0.0067
- D. 0

FE ELECTRICAL AND COMPUTER PRACTICE EXAM

73. The closed-loop, negative feedback control system shown has the transfer function:

$$\frac{C(s)}{R(s)} = \frac{G(s)}{1+G(s)H(s)} = \frac{10s}{s^2+5s+10}$$

If $r(t)$ is a unit step input, the steady-state error $e(t)$ is most nearly:

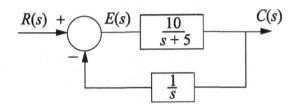

- ○ A.   0
- ○ B.   1
- ○ C.   2
- ○ D.   ∞

74. Consider the unity feedback system:

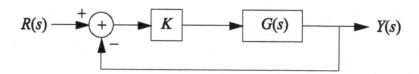

with $G(s) = \dfrac{1}{(s+2)(s+4)}$ and $K > 0$.

On the complex plane below, mark the breakaway point for the root-locus plot for this system.

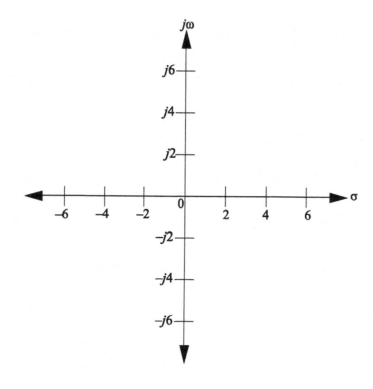

75. The following Routh array has been constructed for a simple control system with a gain of K in the feedback path.

$$\begin{array}{ll} s^4 & 1 \qquad\qquad 12 \qquad\qquad 42K \\ s^3 & 7 \qquad\qquad 10 + 14K \\ s^2 & \dfrac{74 - 14K}{7} \qquad 42K \\ s^1 & \dfrac{196K^2 - 1{,}162K - 740}{14K - 74} \\ s^0 & 42K \end{array}$$

The denominator of the **closed-loop** system transfer function is:

- A. $s^3 + 7s^2 + 12s + 10$
- B. $s^4 + 7s^3 + 12s^2 + 10s$
- C. $s^4 + 7s^3 + 12s^2 + (10 + 14K)s + 42K$
- D. not defined from the Routh array

76. A unity-feedback control system is shown in the figure below.

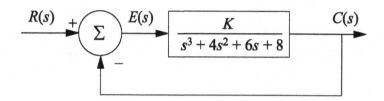

The range of K for which this system is stable is most nearly:

- A. $0 < K < 16$
- B. $8 < K < 16$
- C. $-8 < K < 16$
- D. $-16 < K < -8$

FE ELECTRICAL AND COMPUTER PRACTICE EXAM

77. A signal $x(t) = 1 + 0.8 \sin 50t$ modulates an AM carrier $y(t) = 2 \sin 1{,}000t$ by multiplying the two signals as shown below:

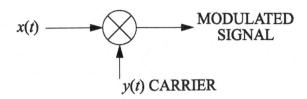

The two-sided magnitude spectrum of the modulated signal is shown below:

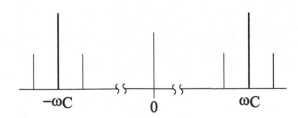

The normalized power (W) into a 1-Ω resistor contained in the signal at 1,050 rad/s is most nearly:

- ○ A.   0.32
- ○ B.   0.64
- ○ C.   0.80
- ○ D.   1.28

78. An amplitude modulation system is shown below in block diagram form.

$m(t) = A_m \cos \omega_m t$
B is a constant bias voltage.
$c(t) = A_c \cos \omega_c t$

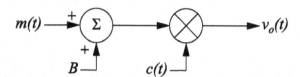

The frequencies found in the output $v_o(t)$ are:

- A. ω_c, ω_m
- B. $\omega_c, \omega_c + \omega_m$
- C. $\omega_c \pm \omega_m$
- D. $\omega_c, \omega_c \pm \omega_m$

79. A portion of a voice communication system is shown below. The audio message $m(t)$ is in the range 20 Hz to 500 Hz. The signal $m(t)$ is used to modulate a cosine carrier signal as illustrated below.

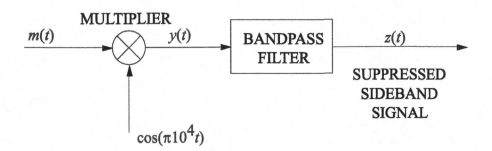

The center frequency and bandwidth, respectively, of an ideal bandpass filter required to suppress the lower sideband and the carrier of $y(t)$ to produce $z(t)$ are most nearly:

- A. 250 Hz, 250 Hz
- B. 0 Hz, 1,000 Hz
- C. 5,250 Hz, 500 Hz
- D. 4,750 Hz, 500 Hz

80. Consider the following signal:

$$x(t) = A \cos[\omega_2 t + \eta \sin \omega_1 t]$$

where $\omega_1 \ll \omega_2$ and η is the modulation index.

If η is a constant and $\sin \omega_1 t$ is the message, the resulting signal $x(t)$ is:

- A. phase modulated (PM)
- B. amplitude modulated (AM)
- C. pulse-width modulated (PWM)
- D. pulse-shift modulated (PSM)

81. A 10-MHz carrier is AM-modulated by a symmetrical square wave with a period of 1 ms. The bandwidth (kHz) of a filter with a center frequency of 10 MHz required to transmit the square wave with the first five nonzero components ($n = 1, 3, 5, 7, 9$) of its Fourier components is most nearly:

- A. 3
- B. 6
- C. 10
- D. 20

82. When data is transmitted in a serial format, an error detection bit called a parity bit may be appended to the bit stream. A serial receiver that uses even parity has received the following nine bits (parity bit followed by eight data bits).

    000110100

    Which statement best describes the received code?

    - A. No errors occurred during transmission.
    - B. An even number of bits have been corrupted during transmission.
    - C. An odd number of bits have been corrupted during transmission.
    - D. A bit transmitted as a one (1) has been changed to a zero (0) during transmission.

83. In data transmission terminology, a *station* refers to a computer, terminal, telephone, or some other communication device. The transmission path connecting a pair of stations is called a channel or link. The links may be simplex, half-duplex, or full-duplex. Assume that there are five stations, and each station is capable of sending or receiving. All stations are fully interconnected with full-duplex links. The number of links required to connect the network is:

    - A. 4
    - B. 5
    - C. 10
    - D. 25

FE ELECTRICAL AND COMPUTER PRACTICE EXAM

84. In computer networks, the function of a router is to:

   ○ A.   connect two or more computers on the same local area network
   ○ B.   connect a computer to the Ethernet
   ○ C.   connect local area networks
   ○ D.   detect collisions of data packets from computers on the network and retransmit them as necessary

85. Most computer networks use packet switching to move data from the transmitting computer to the receiving computer. The following properties apply to packet-switched networks:

   Select **all** that apply.

   ☐ A.   The size of the data blocks is limited.
   ☐ B.   The nth packet of a message may be forwarded before the $(n + 1)$ packet has fully arrived.
   ☐ C.   The path from transmitting to receiving must be established before transmission starts.
   ☐ D.   Packets may be delivered to the destination in the wrong order.
   ☐ E.   The required bandwidth is reserved in advance. Thus, any unused bandwidth is wasted.

86. The transport layer of the OSI framework provides a mechanism for the exchange of data between end systems. Examples of protocols that operate on the transport layer include:

   ○ A.   IP and TCP
   ○ B.   IP and UDP
   ○ C.   TCP and UDP
   ○ D.   IP, TCP, and UDP

FE ELECTRICAL AND COMPUTER PRACTICE EXAM

87. The binary number 1011 corresponds to the decimal number:

- A. 3
- B. 10
- C. 11
- D. 15

88. Which of the following is a binary representation of the base-10 fraction $\frac{93}{128}$?

- A. 0.1011100
- B. 0.1011101
- C. 0.1011110
- D. 0.1011111

89. The K-map below was generated from a logic function F.

C \ AB	00	01	11	10
0	0	1	1	1
1	0	1	0	0

The expression that best represents the logic function F is:

- A. $A\bar{C} + AB$
- B. $\bar{A}C + \bar{A}B$
- C. $A\bar{C} + A\bar{B}$
- D. $A\bar{C} + \bar{A}B$

90. Consider the following Karnaugh map:

AB\CD	00	01	11	10
00	1			1
01	1	1	1	1
11				
10	1			1

Which logic function best represents a minimal SOP expression?

- A. $f(A,B,C,D) = \bar{B}\bar{D} + \bar{A}B + \bar{A}\bar{D}$
- B. $f(A,B,C,D) = \bar{A}\bar{D} + \bar{A}B + A\bar{B}\bar{D}$
- C. $f(A,B,C,D) = \bar{A}\bar{D} + \bar{A}BD + A\bar{B}\bar{D}$
- D. $f(A,B,C,D) = \bar{B}\bar{D} + \bar{A}B$

FE ELECTRICAL AND COMPUTER PRACTICE EXAM

91. Flip-flops *A* and *B* form a sequential synchronous circuit as shown below.

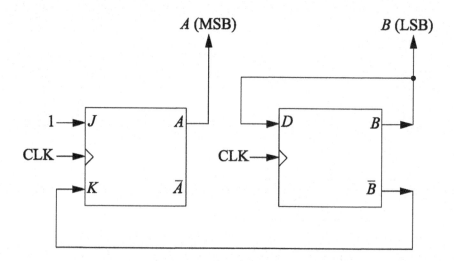

After the clock pulse, binary count 10 (*A* = 1, *B* = 0) changes to:

- A. 00
- B. 01
- C. 10
- D. 11

FE ELECTRICAL AND COMPUTER PRACTICE EXAM

92. A sequential logic circuit has one input (x), one output (z), and six states labeled A–F. The circuit is described by the state table shown below. Entries in the two right-hand columns represent the next-state/output-value combination for each present-state condition and input value. For example, if the present state is B and an input $x = 1$ is applied, the next state will be D and the value of z will be 0.

If the circuit is initially in State C and the input sequence $x = 100$ is applied (meaning the first input is 1, the second input is 0, etc.), the output sequence is best described by:

Present State	Next State/Output Input x	
	0	1
A	C/0	A/0
B	B/1	D/0
C	D/0	B/1
D	F/1	B/1
E	E/1	F/0
F	F/0	A/1

- A. 101
- B. 010
- C. 100
- D. 111

93. An instruction pipeline is a computer design technique that generally improves performance for which of the following reasons?

- A. The time to execute a single instruction is reduced.
- B. A future instruction may be decoded at the same time the current instruction is being executed.
- C. Memory access time is reduced.
- D. The execution operation can be performed on multiple instructions simultaneously.

94. When a CPU fetches an instruction word from memory, the word contains an operation code (op code) that indicates the type of operation the CPU is to perform and information specifying where the instruction operands are located. A computer may use various addressing modes to specify the operand location. One such addressing mode is shown below, where R designates some register within the CPU and d is a constant embedded in the instruction word.

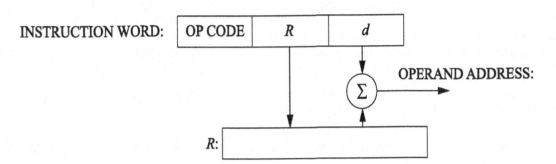

Which of the following terms best describes the addressing mode used by the instruction above?

- A. Immediate addressing
- B. Direct addressing
- C. Indexed addressing
- D. Indirect addressing

FE ELECTRICAL AND COMPUTER PRACTICE EXAM

95. A microprocessor (μp) uses a 16-bit address bus and an 8-bit data bus. The address bus lines are labeled A_{15} to A_0, where A_{15} is the most significant address bit and A_0 is the least significant address bit. The microprocessor generates an active-low address strobe (AS) at the beginning of each memory access cycle to indicate that a valid address has been placed on the address bus. The AS signal is asserted for the entire memory access cycle.

In a certain application of the μp, the three most significant address bits (A_{15}–A_{13}) are used as inputs to a 3-of-8 decoder to generate chip-select signals (CS_0–CS_7). The chip-select signals are used to enable an EPROM memory device whose address lines are tied directly to the lower 13 address lines (A_{12}–A_0) of the μp. The EPROM's output lines are enabled whenever its enable input (EN) is pulled low. A figure of the microprocessor described above and the decoder truth table are shown on the opposite page.

The range of addresses (expressed in hexadecimal) to which the EPROM in the figure will respond is most nearly:

95. (Continued)

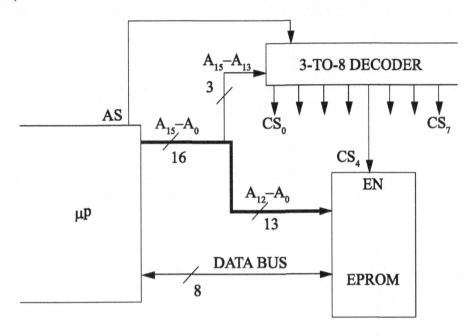

				Decoder Truth Table							
AS	A_{15}	A_{14}	A_{13}	CS_0	CS_1	CS_2	CS_3	CS_4	CS_5	CS_6	CS_7
1	X	X	X	1	1	1	1	1	1	1	1
0	0	0	0	0	1	1	1	1	1	1	1
0	0	0	1	1	0	1	1	1	1	1	1
0	0	1	0	1	1	0	1	1	1	1	1
0	0	1	1	1	1	1	0	1	1	1	1
0	1	0	0	1	1	1	1	0	1	1	1
0	1	0	1	1	1	1	1	1	0	1	1
0	1	1	0	1	1	1	1	1	1	0	1
0	1	1	1	1	1	1	1	1	1	1	0

X = "don't care"

- A. 0000 to 1FFF
- B. 4000 to 5FFF
- C. 8000 to 9FFF
- D. E000 to FFFF

96. A microprocessor uses the instruction format shown for instructions that use a direct address. The amount of memory that can be accessed using direct address mode is most nearly:

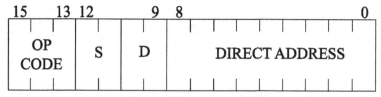

S specifies the source register
D specifies the destination register

- A. 256 words
- B. 512 words
- C. 1,024 words
- D. 2,048 words

97. The flowchart for a computer program contains the following segment:

```
VAR = 0
→ IF VAR < 5 THEN VAR = VAR + 2
  OTHERWISE EXIT LOOP
- LOOP
```

What is the value of VAR at the conclusion of this routine?

- A. 0
- B. 2
- C. 4
- D. 6

98. The following function counts down starting at Y. What number does the countdown return if it is called with Y = 10?

> function countdown (Y)
>   loop while (Y > 0)
>   do Y = Y − 1
>   loop next
>   return Y

- A. −1
- B. 0
- C. 1
- D. 10

99. The final value of Q in the following flowchart is most nearly:

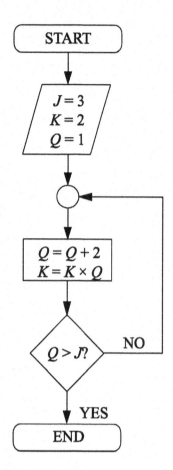

- A. 0
- B. 1
- C. 3
- D. 5

100. The following segment of pseudocode describes a segment of a computer program:

> Set A = 17
> Set K = 2
> While K ≤ 4
>   A = A/K
>   K = K + 1
> End While
> Print A

The value of A that is printed is most nearly:

- A. 0.71
- B. 2.83
- C. 4.25
- D. 408

SOLUTIONS

FE ELECTRICAL AND COMPUTER SOLUTIONS

Detailed solutions for each question begin on the next page.

1	A	26	C	51	B	76	C
2	D	27	B	52	D	77	A
3	C	28	B	53	C	78	D
4	A	29	B	54	A	79	C
5	B	30	B	55	B	80	A
6	D	31	B	56	A	81	D
7	D	32	B	57	A	82	C
8	D	33	A	58	C	83	C
9	A	34	A	59	A	84	C
10	C	35	C	60	A	85	A, B, D
11	C	36	8	61	A	86	C
12	see solution	37	C	62	A	87	C
13	A	38	B	63	A	88	B
14	B	39	A	64	C	89	D
15	C	40	see solution	65	C	90	D
16	B	41	B	66	B	91	A
17	B	42	D	67	B	92	D
18	C	43	D	68	C	93	B
19	C	44	B	69	D	94	C
20	A	45	A	70	B	95	C
21	D	46	D	71	A	96	B
22	B	47	D	72	B	97	D
23	B	48	C	73	A	98	B
24	D	49	D	74	see solution	99	D
25	B	50	A	75	C	100	A

FE ELECTRICAL AND COMPUTER SOLUTIONS

1. Refer to the Mathematics section of the *FE Reference Handbook*.

    $\theta = 180 - 110 - 45 = 25°$

    Law of sines:

    $\dfrac{10}{\sin 110°} = \dfrac{AB}{\sin 25°}$

    AB = 4.497 cm

    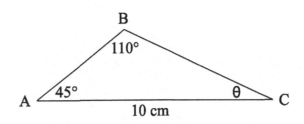

    THE CORRECT ANSWER IS: A

2. $\dfrac{(1-i)^2}{(1+i)^2} = \dfrac{1-2i+i^2}{1+2i+i^2} = \dfrac{1-1-2i}{1-1+2i} = \dfrac{-i}{i} = -1$

    THE CORRECT ANSWER IS: D

3. Refer to the Electrical and Computer Engineering section of the *FE Reference Handbook*.

    $\dfrac{(10+j3)}{(-6+j4)} \dfrac{(-6-j4)}{(-6-j4)} = \dfrac{-60-j40-j18+12}{36+16}$ Rationalize the denominator.

    $= \dfrac{-48-j58}{52}$

    $= -0.923 - j1.12$

    Alternate solution (polar form)

    $A = 10 + j3 = 10.44 \angle 16.70°$

    $B = -6 + j4 = 7.21 \angle 146.31°$

    $\dfrac{A}{B} = \dfrac{10.44 \angle 16.70°}{7.21 \angle 146.31°} = 1.448 \angle -129.61°$

    $= -0.92 - j1.12$

    THE CORRECT ANSWER IS: C

83

FE ELECTRICAL AND COMPUTER SOLUTIONS

4.

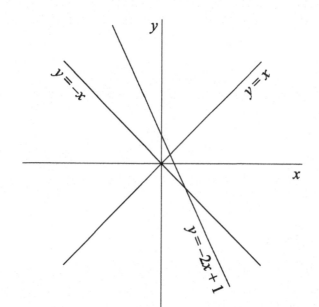

$y = -x$

$y = x$

$y = -2x + 1$

From graph one, the intersection is at (0, 0), so Options C. and D. are incorrect.

Also, the second intersection is at (1, –1), so the vertices are at (0, 0), $\left(\frac{1}{3}, \frac{1}{3}\right)$, (1, –1).

THE CORRECT ANSWER IS: A

5. $f(x) = x^3 + x^2 - 3$

$f'(x) = 3x^2 + 2x$

$f''(x) = 6x + 2$
$6x + 2 = 0$
$x = -1/3$

$f''(x)$ negative below $x = -1/3$
$f''(x)$ positive above $x = -1/3$

Since $f''(x) = 0$ and $f''(x)$ changes sign at $x = -1/3$, the inflection point is at $x = -1/3$.

THE CORRECT ANSWER IS: B

FE ELECTRICAL AND COMPUTER SOLUTIONS

6. Refer to the Mathematics section of the *FE Reference Handbook*.

$$\frac{\partial f}{\partial y} = \frac{\partial(x^2)}{\partial y} + \frac{\partial(xy)}{\partial y} + \frac{\partial(y^2)}{\partial y}$$
$$= 0 + x + 2y$$
$$= x + 2y$$

THE CORRECT ANSWER IS: D

7. $\frac{d^2y}{dt^2} + 6\frac{dy}{dt} + 25y = x(t)$

The characteristic equation is $D^2 + 6D + 25 = 0$

Referring to Second-Order Linear Homogeneous Differential Equations with Constant Coefficients in the Mathematics section of the *FE Reference Handbook*:

$a = 6$
$a^2 = 36$
$b = 25$
$4b = 100$

Since $a^2 = 36$ is less than $4b = 100$, the system is underdamped.

THE CORRECT ANSWER IS: D

FE ELECTRICAL AND COMPUTER SOLUTIONS

8. Refer to Differential Equations in the Mathematics section of the *FE Reference Handbook*. The characteristic equation for a second-order linear homogeneous differential equation is:

$$r^2 + ar + b = 0$$

In this problem, $a = 4$ and $b = 4$

$$r^2 + 4r + 4 = 0$$

In solving the characteristic equation, it is noted that there are repeated real roots: $r_1 = r_2 = -2$

Because $a^2 = 4b$, the solution for this critically damped system is:

$$y(x) = (C_1 + C_2 x) e^{-2x}$$

THE CORRECT ANSWER IS: D

9. Refer to Resolution of a Force in the Statics section of the *FE Reference Handbook*.

$$R_x = \sum F_{xi}, \qquad R_y = \sum F_{yi}, \quad i = 1,2,3$$
$$R_x = 2.12 + 5 \cos 105° = 2.12 - 1.29 = 0.83 \text{ N}$$
$$R_y = 2.12 + 5 \sin 105° = 2.12 + 4.83 = 6.95 \text{ N}$$
$$R = \sqrt{R_x^2 + R_y^2} = \sqrt{0.83^2 + 6.95^2} = 6.999 \text{ N}$$

THE CORRECT ANSWER IS: A

FE ELECTRICAL AND COMPUTER SOLUTIONS

10. The cross product of vectors **A** and **B** is a vector perpendicular to **A** and **B**.

$$\begin{vmatrix} \mathbf{i} & \mathbf{j} & \mathbf{k} \\ 2 & 4 & 0 \\ 1 & 1 & -1 \end{vmatrix} = \mathbf{i}(-4) - \mathbf{j}(-2 - 0) + \mathbf{k}(2 - 4) = -4\mathbf{i} + 2\mathbf{j} - 2\mathbf{k}$$

To obtain a unit vector, divide by the magnitude.

$$\text{Magnitude} = \sqrt{(-4)^2 + 2^2 + (-2)^2} = \sqrt{24} = 2\sqrt{6}$$

$$\frac{-4\mathbf{i} + 2\mathbf{j} - 2\mathbf{k}}{2\sqrt{6}} = \frac{-2\mathbf{i} + \mathbf{j} - \mathbf{k}}{\sqrt{6}}$$

THE CORRECT ANSWER IS: C

11. From the Dispersion, Mean, Median and Mode Values in the Mathematics section of the *FE Reference Handbook*:

There are eight measurements. The fourth and fifth measurements are 11 and 12. Since the number of items (eight) is even, the median is the average of the fourth and fifth measurements.

$$\text{Median} = \frac{11 + 12}{2} = 11.5$$

THE CORRECT ANSWER IS: C

FE ELECTRICAL AND COMPUTER SOLUTIONS

12.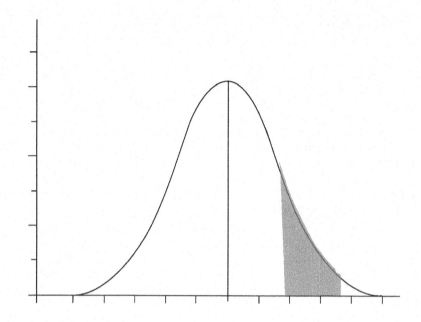

THE CORRECT ANSWER IS SHADED ABOVE.

13. $Z = \dfrac{15.5 - 8.0}{2.5} = 3.0$

From the Unit Normal Distribution table in the Engineering Probability and Statistics section of the *FE Reference Handbook*.

For $x = 3$, $R(x) = 0.0013$

THE CORRECT ANSWER IS: A

FE ELECTRICAL AND COMPUTER SOLUTIONS

14. Refer to the Engineering Probability and Statistics section of the *FE Reference Handbook.*

Binomial distribution
$p = 0.5$ (chance of getting a head)
$q = 0.5$ (chance of not getting a head)
$n = 10$ (number of trials)
$x = 4$ (number of heads)

$$P_{10}(4) = \frac{10!}{4!6!}(0.5^4)(0.5^6) = \frac{(10)(9)(8)(7)}{(4)(3)(2)(1)}(0.5)^{10}$$

$$= 0.2051$$

THE CORRECT ANSWER IS: B

15. Refer to the NCEES Rules of Professional Conduct, Section B, in the Ethics section of the *FE Reference Handbook.*

THE CORRECT ANSWER IS: C

16. Refer to the NCEES Rules of Professional Conduct, Section A.4., in the Ethics section of the *FE Reference Handbook.*

THE CORRECT ANSWER IS: B

17. Refer to the NCEES Rules of Professional Conduct, Section A, in the Ethics section of the *FE Reference Handbook.*

THE CORRECT ANSWER IS: B

18. Refer to the Ethics section of the *FE Reference Handbook.* Section B in the Rules of Professional Conduct states:

"Licensees shall undertake assignments only when qualified by education or experience in the specific technical fields of engineering or surveying involved."

THE CORRECT ANSWER IS: C

FE ELECTRICAL AND COMPUTER SOLUTIONS

19. Refer to Non-annual Compounding in the Engineering Economics section of the *FE Reference Handbook*. Use the non-annual compounding interest equation:

$$i_e = \left(1 + \frac{r}{m}\right)^m - 1$$

$r = 0.17 \; m = 4$

$$i_e = \left(1 + \frac{0.17}{4}\right)^4 - 1$$

$$= 0.1815$$

THE CORRECT ANSWER IS: C

20. Annual cost: $= \$900(A/P, 8\%, 5) + \$50 - \$300(A/F, 8\%, 5)$
    $= \$900(0.2505) + \$50 - \$300(0.1705)$
    $= \$225.45 + \$50 - \$51.15$
    $= \$224.30$

THE CORRECT ANSWER IS: A

FE ELECTRICAL AND COMPUTER SOLUTIONS

21.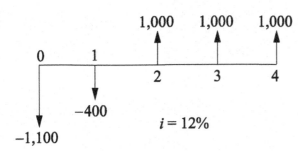

$P = -1{,}100 - 400\,(P/F, 12\%, 1) + 1{,}000\,(P/F, 12\%, 2) + 1{,}000\,(P/F, 12\%, 3) + 1{,}000\,(P/F, 12\%, 4)$

$= -1{,}100 - 400\,(0.8929) + 1{,}000\,(0.7972) + 1{,}000\,(0.7118) + 1{,}000\,(0.6355)$

$= 687.34$

$A = P\,(A/P, 12\%, 4) = 687.34(0.3292)$

$= \$226$ per year

THE CORRECT ANSWER IS: D

22. Refer to the definition of break-even analysis in the Engineering Economics section of the *FE Reference Handbook*.

THE CORRECT ANSWER IS: B

23. Refer to the Chemistry section of the *FE Reference Handbook*.

Oxidation is defined as the loss of electrons. In this case, $Cu^{2+} \rightarrow Cu$, which gains two electrons, and $Zn \rightarrow Zn^{2+}$, which loses two electrons. Therefore, only zinc is oxidized.

THE CORRECT ANSWER IS: B

24. See the Standard Oxidation Potentials for Corrosion Reactions table in the Chemistry section of the *FE Reference Handbook*. Zn has a higher electromotive potential and would protect Fe.

THE CORRECT ANSWER IS: D

FE ELECTRICAL AND COMPUTER SOLUTIONS

25. Refer to the Chemistry section of the *FE Reference Handbook.*

    The table of Standard Oxidation Potentials shows that aluminum is anodic relative to copper and, therefore, will corrode to protect the copper.

    THE CORRECT ANSWER IS: B

26. Refer to the Electrical and Computer Section of the *FE Reference Handbook.*

    Since the current density is 100 A/m^2, the current in the conductor is given by:
    $I = 100 \times \text{Area} = 100 \times (\pi r^2) = 100 \times \pi (0.05)^2$
    $I = 0.7854 \text{ A}$

    The resistance per unit length is given by:

    $R = \dfrac{\rho L}{A} = \dfrac{0.1 \, \Omega \cdot m \times L}{\pi (0.05 \, m)^2} = 12.73 \, \Omega/m$

    Since $P = I^2 R$, the power loss per unit length is given by:

    $P = (0.785 \text{A})^2 \times 12.73 \, \Omega/m = 7.854 \text{ W/m}$

    THE CORRECT ANSWER IS: C

27. The power dissipated in a resistor can be found by applying the equation $P = \dfrac{V^2}{R}$.

    The voltage across the 90-Ω resistor is 100 − 60 = 40 V. Therefore, $P = \dfrac{40^2}{90 \, \Omega} = 17.78 \text{ W}$

    THE CORRECT ANSWER IS: B

FE ELECTRICAL AND COMPUTER SOLUTIONS

28. Initially, $V_C(t) = 150$ V

$$W_C(t) = \frac{1}{2}CV_C^2 = \frac{1}{2}(10 \times 10^{-6}\,\text{F})(150\,\text{V})^2$$

$W_C = 0.113$ J initial stored energy.

After ten time constants, all energy will be dissipated.

THE CORRECT ANSWER IS: B

29. Refer to Electrostatics in the Electrical and Computer Engineering section of the *FE Reference Handbook*.

$$\mathbf{F}_2 = \frac{Q_1 Q_2}{4\pi\varepsilon r^2}\mathbf{a}_{r12},$$

where: $\mathbf{F}_2$ = force (N)
  $Q_1 = 5$ C
  $Q_2 = -12$ C
  $\varepsilon = \varepsilon_o = 8.85 \times 10^{-12}$ F/m
  r = distance (m) between the two point charges
  $\mathbf{a}_{r12}$ = unit vector (neglected in this case because only two spheres are involved)

$$\mathbf{F}_2 = \frac{(5)(-12)}{4\pi(8.85\times 10^{-12})\left(\frac{30}{100}\right)^2} = -6\times 10^{12}\,\text{N}$$

THE CORRECT ANSWER IS: B

FE ELECTRICAL AND COMPUTER SOLUTIONS

30. All of the potential energy at rest is converted to kinetic energy at the anode.

P.E. = K.E.

$q_e(\Delta V) = 1/2 \, m_e \, v^2$

$(1.6 \times 10^{-19})(2 \times 10^4) = 1/2 \, (9.1 \times 10^{-31}) \, v^2$

$v^2 = 7 \times 10^{15}$

$v = 83.9 \times 10^6$ m/s

THE CORRECT ANSWER IS: B

31. Refer to the Electrical and Computer Section of the *FE Reference Handbook*.

$W = Q \int_a^b \overline{E} \cdot d\overline{l} = -Q\overline{E} \cdot \overline{l} = -3.25 \times 10^{-6} (2\overline{a}_x + 3\overline{a}_y + 4\overline{a}_z) \cdot (-5\overline{a}_x + 0\overline{a}_y + 3\overline{a}_z)$

$= -3.25 \times 10^{-6} \times 2 = -6.5 \times 10^{-6}$

THE CORRECT ANSWER IS: B

32. At $t = 0$, $V_c = 60 \times \dfrac{2}{2+1} = 40$ V, the energy stored in the capacitor at $t = 0$ is:

$W_c = 1/2 \, C \, V_c^2 = 1/2 \, (10 \, \mu F)(40 \, V)^2$

$W_c = 5 \times 10^{-6} \, (1{,}600)$

$W_c = 8$ mJ

The 2-kΩ resistor dissipates $\dfrac{2}{2+3} = 40\%$ of W_c or 3.2 mJ

THE CORRECT ANSWER IS: B

FE ELECTRICAL AND COMPUTER SOLUTIONS

33. Apply KCL to the node marked V_O:

$$\frac{1}{3}(V_O - 36) + \frac{1}{6}V_O + \frac{1}{6}(V_O - 6) = 0 \Rightarrow V_O = 19.5 \text{ V}$$

THE CORRECT ANSWER IS: A

34. $R_T = 4\,\Omega + 3\,\Omega \parallel 6\,\Omega = 4\,\Omega + 2\,\Omega$

$R_T = 6\,\Omega \Rightarrow I_T = \dfrac{6\text{ V}}{6\,\Omega} = 1\text{ A}$

$I_x = \dfrac{3}{9}(I_T) = \dfrac{1}{3}\text{ A}$

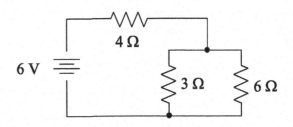

THE CORRECT ANSWER IS: A

FE ELECTRICAL AND COMPUTER SOLUTIONS

35. Refer to the Electrical and Computer Engineering section of the *FE Reference Handbook*.

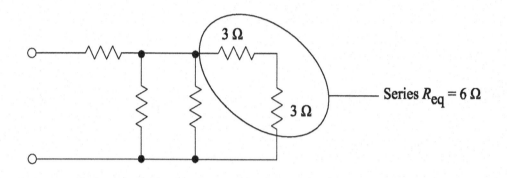

Series $R_{eq} = 6\,\Omega$

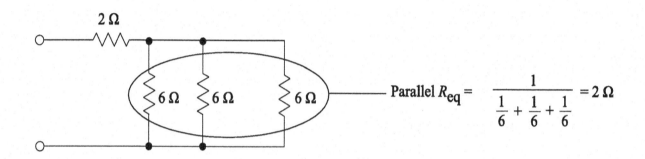

Parallel $R_{eq} = \dfrac{1}{\dfrac{1}{6} + \dfrac{1}{6} + \dfrac{1}{6}} = 2\,\Omega$

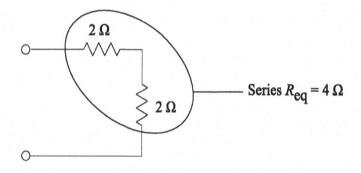

Series $R_{eq} = 4\,\Omega$

THE CORRECT ANSWER IS: C

FE ELECTRICAL AND COMPUTER SOLUTIONS

36. If $i_1 = 1.25$ mA, then the total resistance i_1 can see must be $\dfrac{10 \text{ V}}{1.25 \text{ mA}} = 8 \text{ k}\Omega$

$$4,000 + \frac{R(4,000 + 4,000)}{R + 4,000 + 4,000} = 8,000 \ \Omega$$

$$\frac{8,000R}{8,000 + R} = 4,000 \ \Omega$$

$$8,000R = 4,000R + 32 \text{ M}\Omega$$

$$R = 32 \text{ M}\Omega / 4 \text{ k}\Omega$$

$$= 8 \text{ k}\Omega$$

THE CORRECT ANSWER IS: 8

37. R_N is the total resistance seen at the load end with the voltage source set equal to zero (replaced by short circuit).

$R_N = 60 \ \Omega + (50 \ \Omega$ in parallel with $200 \ \Omega)$

$R_N = 60 + 40 = 100 \ \Omega$

THE CORRECT ANSWER IS: C

38. With the 12-V source zeroed (short), $R_{Th} = 8 + 12 \parallel 6 = 8 + 4 = 12 \ \Omega$

Alternate Solution:

$$R_{eq} = \frac{V_{oc}}{I_{sc}}$$

$$V_{oc} = 12 \cdot \left(\frac{12}{6+12}\right) = 8$$

$$I_{sc} = \frac{12}{6 + \left(\dfrac{8 \cdot 12}{8+12}\right)} \cdot \left(\frac{12}{8+12}\right) = 0.666$$

$$R_{eq} = \frac{8}{0.666} = 12 \ \Omega$$

THE CORRECT ANSWER IS: B

FE ELECTRICAL AND COMPUTER SOLUTIONS

39. Refer to Effective or RMS Values in the Electrical and Computer section of the *FE Reference Handbook*.

$$X_{rms} = \sqrt{X_{dc}^2 + \sum_{n=1}^{\infty} X_n^2}$$

for i_1 $X_{rms} = \sqrt{0^2 + \left[\left(\frac{10}{\sqrt{2}}\right)^2 + \left(\frac{-7}{\sqrt{2}}\right)^2 + \left(\frac{-3}{\sqrt{2}}\right)^2\right]} = 8.89$

for i_2 $X_{rms} = \sqrt{0^2 + \left[\left(\frac{10}{\sqrt{2}}\right)^2 + \left(\frac{3}{\sqrt{2}}\right)^2 + \left(\frac{7}{\sqrt{2}}\right)^2\right]} = 8.89$

Thus both waveforms have the same rms value.

THE CORRECT ANSWER IS: A

FE ELECTRICAL AND COMPUTER SOLUTIONS

40. Refer to the Electrical and Computer Engineering Section of the *FE Reference Handbook*.

Time domain:

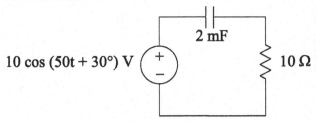

From the sinusoidal source, $\omega = 50$ rad/sec

$$Z_C = \frac{1}{j\omega C} = -j\frac{1}{50(0.002)} = -j10 \ \Omega$$

$$Z_R = R = 10 \ \Omega$$

$$V_S = V_M \angle \phi = 10\angle 30° \ V$$

∴ in Frequency (Phasor) domain

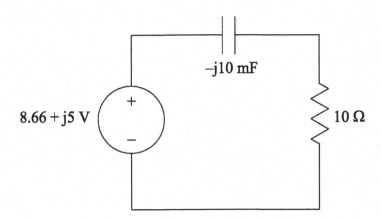

THE CORRECT ANSWER IS SHOWN ABOVE.

99

FE ELECTRICAL AND COMPUTER SOLUTIONS

41. Refer to the Electrical and Computer Engineering section of the *FE Reference Handbook*.

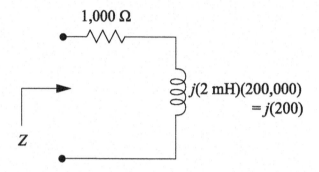

The impedance of the resistor is $Z_R = R = 1,000 \ \Omega$.
The impedance of the inductor is $Z_L = j\omega L = j(100,000)(0.002) = j200 \ \Omega$
Since they are in series, $Z = 1,000 + j200 \ \Omega$

THE CORRECT ANSWER IS: B

42. $Z = 30 + j90 - j50 = 30 + j40 \ \Omega$

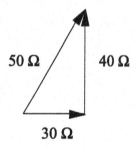

THE CORRECT ANSWER IS: D

FE ELECTRICAL AND COMPUTER SOLUTIONS

43. Reference RC and RL Transients in the *FE Reference Handbook*.

After a long time, $v_c = 60 \times \dfrac{2}{2+1} = 40$ V

After $t = 0^+$,

$$v_c(t) = v_c(0)e^{\frac{-t}{RC}}$$

$RC = 5\text{ k}\Omega \times 10\text{ }\mu\text{F} = 5{,}000 \times 10^{-5} = 0.05$

$$v_c(t) = 40\, e^{\frac{-t}{0.05}} = 40\, e^{-20t}$$

THE CORRECT ANSWER IS: D

44. v_O will be maximum when L and C are in parallel resonance.

$$\omega_o = \dfrac{1}{\sqrt{LC}} = \dfrac{1}{\sqrt{(0.5 \times 10^{-6})(5 \times 10^{-3})}} = \dfrac{1}{\sqrt{25 \times 10^{-10}}}$$

$$= \dfrac{10^5}{5} = 2 \times 10^4 \text{ rad/s} \qquad f_o = \dfrac{20 \times 10^3}{2\pi} = 3.18 \text{ kHz}$$

THE CORRECT ANSWER IS: B

45.

$$Z_{in} = \dfrac{V_i}{I_i} = R_1 + \dfrac{1}{sC_1} + \dfrac{\dfrac{R_2}{sC_2}}{R_2 + \dfrac{1}{sC_2}}$$

$$= \dfrac{sR_1C_1 + 1}{sC_1} + \dfrac{R_2}{sR_2C_2 + 1}$$

$$= \dfrac{(sR_1C_1 + 1)(sR_2C_2 + 1) + sR_2C_1}{R_2C_1C_2\left[s\left(s + \dfrac{1}{R_2C_2}\right)\right]}$$

Poles at $s = 0$; $s = -\dfrac{1}{R_2C_2}$

THE CORRECT ANSWER IS: A

46. $$V_{out}(s) = \frac{1.2(s+2)}{(s+1)(s+4)}\left(\frac{1}{s}\right)$$

Applying the final value theorem to this, we multiply by s, which cancels s in the denominator.

Evaluate $\frac{V_{out}}{V_{in}}$ at $s = 0 \Rightarrow \frac{1.2 \times 2}{4} = 0.6 \Rightarrow V_{out}(\infty) = 0.6(1) = 0.6$ V

Alternatively, by inspection of the circuit with each capacitance replaced with an open circuit:

$$\frac{30}{30+20} = 0.6 \text{ V}$$

THE CORRECT ANSWER IS: D

47. For $0 < t < 1$

$$x(t) * h(t) = \int_0^t (\lambda)(1) d\lambda = \frac{1}{2}t^2$$

This is a quadratic. Only the figure shown in Option D is quadratic for $0 < t < 1$.

THE CORRECT ANSWER IS: D

48. The function $x(t) = t$ for the time range $0 \leq t \leq 1$ and $h(t) = 1$. The convolution integral is:

$$y(t) = \int_0^t h(\lambda - t) x(\lambda) d\lambda = \int_0^t \lambda d\lambda = t^2/2$$

THE CORRECT ANSWER IS: C

49. $y[k] = \frac{1}{6}(3x[k] + 2x[k-1] + x[k-2])$

Taking the z-transform of both sides yields:

$$Y(z) = \frac{1}{6}\left[3X(z) + 2z^{-1}X(z) + z^{-2}X(z)\right] = \frac{X(z)}{6}\left[3 + 2z^{-1} + z^{-2}\right] = \frac{X(z)}{6}\left[\frac{3z^2 + 2z + 1}{z^2}\right]$$

$$H(z) = \frac{Y(z)}{X(z)} = \frac{1}{6}\left[\frac{3z^2 + 2z + 1}{z^2}\right]$$

THE CORRECT ANSWER IS: D

50. The value of the integral is

$$\int_{-\infty}^{\infty} \cos(2t)\delta(t-1)dt = \cos(2) = -0.4161.$$

THE CORRECT ANSWER IS: A

51. **THE CORRECT ANSWER IS: B**

52. $V_T = \frac{kT}{q} = \frac{1.38 \times 10^{-23} \text{ J/K} \times 273.15 \text{ K}}{1.6022 \times 10^{-19} \text{ C}} = 23.52 \times 10^{-3}$ V

THE CORRECT ANSWER IS: D

53. $v_{GS} = 1$ V   and $v_{GD} = 0$ V $\Rightarrow v_{DS} = 1$ V

Since $v_{GS} > V_p$ and $v_{GD} > V_p$
      $(1 > -4)$ $(0 > -4)$

the MOSFET operates in the triode region

$\therefore i_D = 0.2[2(1-(-4))(1) - (1)^2] = 0.2[9] = 1.8$ mA

THE CORRECT ANSWER IS: C

54. $I_D = \dfrac{I_{DSS}}{V_p^2}(v_{GS} - V_p)^2$

$4 = \dfrac{16}{16}(v_{GS} + 4)^2 \Rightarrow v_{GS}^2 + 8v_{GS} + 12 = 0$

$v_{GS} = -2, -6$

$-6 < V_p \Rightarrow v_{GS} = -2.0 \text{ V}$

THE CORRECT ANSWER IS: A

55. For dc bias calculations, all capacitors act like open circuits. The Thevenin equivalent of the base-bias circuit can be represented as shown below:

where, $R_B = R_1 \parallel R_2 = 2 \text{ k}\Omega \parallel 1 \text{ k}\Omega = 667 \text{ }\Omega$

$V_{BB} = V_{CC} \dfrac{R_2}{R_1 + R_2} = (30 \text{ V})\left(\dfrac{1 \text{ k}\Omega}{3 \text{ k}\Omega}\right) = 10 \text{ V}$

by KVL: $V_{BB} - I_B R_B - V_{BE} - I_E R_E = 0$

Since $I_B = \dfrac{I_E}{\beta + 1}$

$V_{BB} - \dfrac{I_E}{\beta + 1} R_B - V_{BE} - I_E R_E = 0$

$I_C \approx I_E = \dfrac{V_{BB} - V_{BE}}{R_E + \left(R_B/\beta + 1\right)} \approx \dfrac{V_{BB} - V_{BE}}{R_E} = \dfrac{9.3}{0.5 \text{ k}\Omega} = 18.6 \text{ mA}$

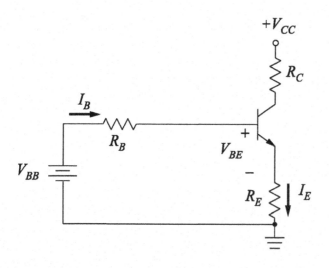

THE CORRECT ANSWER IS: B

56. Since β is large, $V_B \simeq \dfrac{20 \text{ k}\Omega}{100 \text{ k}\Omega} \times 10 \text{ V} = 2 \text{ V}$

$V_E = V_B - V_{BE} = 2 - 0.7 = 1.3 \text{ V}$

$\therefore I_E = \dfrac{1.3 \text{ V}}{1.3 \text{ k}\Omega} \simeq I_C = 1 \text{ mA}$

$V_c = V_{cc} - I_c R_c = 10 \text{ V} - (1 \text{ mA})(4 \text{ k}\Omega) = 6 \text{ V}$

THE CORRECT ANSWER IS: A

57. The input current to an ideal op amp is zero, and the voltage between the two input terminals of an ideal op amp must be zero. Therefore, the voltage divider relation gives

$V_{in} = \left(\dfrac{4}{30+4}\right) V_{out}$

$\dfrac{V_{out}}{V_{in}} = \dfrac{34}{4} = 8.5$

THE CORRECT ANSWER IS: A

FE ELECTRICAL AND COMPUTER SOLUTIONS

58. With V_1 grounded, the circuit is configured as a non-inverting amplifier and

$$V_o = \left(1 + \frac{R_2}{R_1}\right) V_n$$

Where V_n is the voltage applied to the non-inverting terminal of the op amp. V_n can be found by applying the voltage divider rule:

$$V_n = \frac{R_4}{R_3 + R_4} V_2$$

Combining the two results yields:

$$V_o = \left(1 + \frac{R_2}{R_1}\right)\left(\frac{R_4}{R_3 + R_4}\right) V_2$$

$$\frac{V_o}{V_2} = \left(1 + \frac{200\,k\Omega}{5\,k\Omega}\right)\left(\frac{200\,k\Omega}{5\,k\Omega + 200\,k\Omega}\right)$$

$$\frac{V_o}{V_2} = 40$$

THE CORRECT ANSWER IS: C

59. $\mathbf{V}_{AB} = \mathbf{V}_{AN} - \mathbf{V}_{BN} = 100\angle 0° - 100\angle 240° = 173.2\angle 30°$

THE CORRECT ANSWER IS: A

60. $n_s = \dfrac{120 f}{p}$

for $p = 2 \Rightarrow n_s = \dfrac{(120)(60)}{2} = 3{,}600$ rpm

for $p = 4 \Rightarrow n_s = \dfrac{(120)(60)}{4} = 1{,}800$ rpm

$n = (\text{slip})\, n_s$ where $0 < \text{slip} < 1 \Rightarrow n \leq n_s$

n is given as 3,500 rpm $\Rightarrow n = 2$

THE CORRECT ANSWER IS: A

FE ELECTRICAL AND COMPUTER SOLUTIONS

61. The equation for complex power can be found in Complex Power in the Electrical and Computer Engineering section of the *FE Reference Handbook*.

$P_{in} = VI\cos\theta$

$P_{out} = P_{in} \times \text{efficiency} = P_{in} \times 0.85$

$P_{out} = 10 \text{ hp} \times 745.7 \dfrac{W}{hp} = 7.5 \text{ kW} \Rightarrow P_{in} = \dfrac{7.5 \text{ kW}}{0.85} = 8.8 \text{ kW}$

$I = \dfrac{P_{in}}{V\cos\theta} = \dfrac{8.8 \text{ kW}}{440 \text{ V} \times 0.6} = 33.2 \text{ A}$

THE CORRECT ANSWER IS: A

62. $n_s = \dfrac{120 f}{p}$

for $p = 2 \Rightarrow n_s = \dfrac{(120)(60)}{2} = 3{,}600 \text{ rpm}$

for $p = 4 \Rightarrow n_s = \dfrac{(120)(60)}{4} = 1{,}800 \text{ rpm}$

$n = (\text{slip})\, n_s \quad \text{where } 0 < \text{slip} < 1 \Rightarrow n \leq n_s$

n is given as $3{,}500 \text{ rpm} \Rightarrow p = 2$

THE CORRECT ANSWER IS: A

63. $S_1 = 20 \angle 36.87° = 16 + j12 \text{ kVA}$

$S_2 = 10 \angle -53.13° = 6 - j8 \text{ kVA}$

$S = S_1 + S_2 = (16 + j12) + (6 - j8)$

$S = 22 + j4 = P + jQ \Rightarrow Q = 4 \text{ kVAR}$

THE CORRECT ANSWER IS: A

FE ELECTRICAL AND COMPUTER SOLUTIONS

64. Refer to Complex Power in the Electrical and Computer Engineering section of the *FE Reference Handbook* for the equation:

$$P = V_{rms}I_{rms}\cos\theta$$

$$\text{p.f.} = \cos\theta = \frac{P}{V_{rms}I_{rms}}$$

$$= \frac{1{,}500}{(115)(15)}$$

$$= 0.87$$

THE CORRECT ANSWER IS: C

65. Complex ac power is expressed as $\mathbf{S} = P + jQ$, where $P = |\mathbf{S}|\cos\theta$, $Q = |\mathbf{S}|\sin\theta$, and $\theta = \cos^{-1}(\text{pf})$.

The original real and reactive power, then, are given by

$P = 100 \text{ kVA} \times 0.65 = 65 \text{ kW}$ and $Q = 100 \text{ kVA} \times \sin(\cos^{-1} 0.6) = 76 \text{ kVAR}$, inductive

$\mathbf{S}_{ORIGINAL} = 65 \text{ kW} + j76 \text{ kVAR}$

Adding a purely capacitive load will not change the total real power (P), but it will decrease the reactive power (Q).

$\mathbf{S}_{NEW} = 65 \text{ kW} + j(76 - Q_C) \text{ kVAR}$

$$\tan(\theta_{NEW}) = \tan(\cos^{-1} 0.9) = 0.48 = \frac{76 - Q_C}{65} \quad \Rightarrow \quad Q_C = 44.5 \text{ kVAR}$$

THE CORRECT ANSWER IS: C

FE ELECTRICAL AND COMPUTER SOLUTIONS

66. S = apparent power
    P = real power
    Q = reactive power

    $S = P + jQ = |S|\cos\theta + j|S|\sin\theta$

    $\cos\theta = \text{pf} = 0.866$

    $Q = (1{,}500 \text{ VA})\sin[\cos^{-1} 0.866] = 750 \text{ VAR}$

    THE CORRECT ANSWER IS: B

67. Refer to the Magnetic Fields section in the *FE Reference Handbook*.

    $B = \mu H = \dfrac{\mu I}{2\pi r}$

    $I = \dfrac{2\pi r B}{\mu}$

    $= \dfrac{(2\pi)(0.5)(1)}{4\pi(10^{-7})}$

    $= \dfrac{1}{4(10^{-7})}$

    $= 2.5 \times 10^6 \text{ A}$

    THE CORRECT ANSWER IS: B

68. $Z_0 = \sqrt{L/C} \Rightarrow (50)^2 = L/C$

    Therefore $L = 2{,}500 \times 133 \text{ pF/m} = 0.33 \text{ }\mu\text{H/m}$

    THE CORRECT ANSWER IS: C

FE ELECTRICAL AND COMPUTER SOLUTIONS

69.

[Circuit diagram: Voltage source V_S connected through a $j100\,\Omega$ inductor to input terminals with V_{IN}, I_{IN}; transmission line to load with V_L, I_L, and impedance Z_L.]

For a matched lossless transmission line ($Z_L = Z_0$), $V_{IN} = V_L$ and $I_{IN} = I_L$.

$V_{IN} = 200\ V_{rms}$
$I_{IN} = (200/50) = 4\ A_{rms}$
KVL around the loop:
$\quad -V_S + 4(j100) + 200 = 0$
$\quad \therefore V_S = 200 + j400$

$|V_S|_{rms} = \sqrt{200^2 + 400^2} = 447.2\ V_{rms}$

THE CORRECT ANSWER IS: D

70. $Z_0 = \sqrt{L/C}$

$C = \dfrac{L}{Z_0^2} = \dfrac{5\ mH/m}{\left(50\dfrac{V}{A}\right)^2}$

$= 2\ \mu F/m$

THE CORRECT ANSWER IS: B

71. The Bode plot has slopes of 0 dB or –20 dB per decade, so there are simple poles only at $\omega = 10$ rad/s and 1,000 rad/s and a simple zero at $\omega = 100$ rad/s. The only transfer function that satisfies these conditions is Option A.

THE CORRECT ANSWER IS: A

72. $$\frac{Y(s)}{R(s)} = \frac{K}{s^2+2s+150} = \frac{50}{s^2+2\zeta\omega_n s+\omega_n^2}$$

$\therefore \omega_n^2 = 150$ and $2\zeta\omega_n = 2 \Rightarrow \zeta = \frac{2}{2\omega_n} = \frac{1}{\sqrt{150}} = 0.082$

THE CORRECT ANSWER IS: B

73. $$\frac{E(s)}{R(s)} = \frac{1}{1+GH} = \frac{1}{1+10/s(s+5)} = \frac{s(s+5)}{s^2+5s+10}$$

Using the final value theorem and $R(s) = 1/s$:

$$e(t)\Big|_{t\to\infty} = sE(s)\Big|_{s\to 0} = s\left[\frac{s(s+5)}{s^2+5s+10}\right]\frac{1}{s}\Bigg|_{s\to 0} = \frac{s(s+5)}{s^2+5s+10}\Bigg|_{s\to 0} = 0$$

THE CORRECT ANSWER IS: A

FE ELECTRICAL AND COMPUTER SOLUTIONS

74. The characteristic equation for this system is $1 + G(s) = 1 + \dfrac{K}{(s+2)(s+4)}$, which can be written as $K = -(s+2)(s+4)$. Thus, the poles for this equation are at $s = -2$ and -4. The breakaway point will be midway between the poles at $s = -3$.

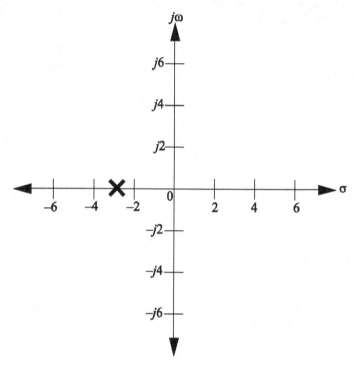

THE CORRECT ANSWER IS MARKED WITH AN X ON THE FIGURE.

75. From the given array, this is a fourth-order system. The denominator of the system is of the form:

$$a_0 s^4 + a_1 s^3 + a_2 s^2 + a_3 s + a_4$$

The Routh array is formed by:

$$\begin{array}{l} s^4 \quad a_0 \; a_2 \; a_4 \\ s^3 \quad a_1 \; a_3 \\ s^2 \quad \dfrac{a_1 a_2 - a_0 a_3}{a_1} \; a_4 \\ \vdots \end{array}$$

Substituting from the given Routh array yields the denominator polynomial:

$$s^4 + 7s^3 + 12s^2 + (10 + 14K)s + 42K$$

THE CORRECT ANSWER IS: C

FE ELECTRICAL AND COMPUTER SOLUTIONS

76. The closed-loop characteristic equation is:

$s^3 + 4s^2 + 6s + 8 + K = 0$

Routh Array

s^3	1	6
s^2	4	$8+K$
s^1	$\dfrac{24-8-K}{4}$	
s^0	$8+K$	

From the first column, $-8 < K < 16$

THE CORRECT ANSWER IS: C

77. The modulated signal, $x(t)$, is given by:

$x(t) = [1 + 0.8 \sin 50t] \times 2 \sin 1{,}000t = 2 \sin 1{,}000t + 1.6 \sin 50t \sin 1{,}000t$
$= 2 \sin 1{,}000t + 0.8 [\cos 950t - \cos 1{,}050t]$

$P = \dfrac{V_{rms}^2}{R}$ and $V_{rms} = \dfrac{V_{peak}}{\sqrt{2}}$

$V_{rms}^2 = \left(\dfrac{0.8}{\sqrt{2}}\right)^2 = 0.32$

$P = \dfrac{0.32}{R} \text{ W}$

The normalized power (into a 1-Ω resistor), then, is 0.32 W.

THE CORRECT ANSWER IS: A

FE ELECTRICAL AND COMPUTER SOLUTIONS

78. Inputs to multiplier are $(B + A_m \cos \omega_m t)$ and $(A_c \cos \omega_c t)$.

Using trigonometric identity:
$$v_0(t) = (B + A_m \cos \omega_m t)(A_c \cos \omega_c t)$$
$$= BA_c \cos \omega_c t + \frac{A_m A_c}{2} \cos(\omega_c + \omega_m)t + \frac{A_m A_c}{2} \cos(\omega_c - \omega_m)t$$

THE CORRECT ANSWER IS: D

79. Center frequency $f_c = 5{,}000 + (500 - 20)/2 = 5{,}240$ Hz $\cong 5{,}250$ Hz

Bandwidth BW $= 500 - 20 = 480 \cong 500$ Hz

THE CORRECT ANSWER IS: C

80. Refer to the phase-deviation equation in the Electrical and Computer Engineering section of the *FE Reference Handbook*.

THE CORRECT ANSWER IS: A

FE ELECTRICAL AND COMPUTER SOLUTIONS

81.

$f(t) \longrightarrow \bigotimes \longrightarrow y(t) = f(t)\cos(\omega_c t)$

$\cos(\omega_c t), \quad \omega_c = 20\pi \times 10^6$ rad/sec

The input signal $f(t)$ is a square wave with period $T = 1$ ms. The Fourier series expansion of $f(t)$ is given by:

$$f(t) = \sum_{\substack{n=1 \\ n \text{ odd}}}^{\infty} (-1)^{(n-1)/2} \frac{4V_0}{n\pi} \cos(n\omega_0 t)$$

where $\omega_0 = \dfrac{2\pi}{T} = \dfrac{2\pi}{1\text{ms}} = 2\pi \times 10^3$ rad/sec

$f_0 = 1$ kHz

The signal $y(t)$ will contain frequency components at $f_c \pm f_0, f_c \pm 3f_0, f_c \pm 5f_0, \ldots$

If the first five nonzero components are to be passed by the filter, the bandwidth of the filter must be $\geq 2 \times 9$ kHz $= 18$ kHz.

THE CORRECT ANSWER IS: D

82. Since the system uses even parity, an even number of "1" bits (including the parity bit) should be received.

An odd number of bits have to be corrupted to detect an error. Since an odd number of bits have been received $\Rightarrow$ 1 or 3 or 5 or ... bits have been corrupted.

THE CORRECT ANSWER IS: C

83. A fully connected network requires $N(N-1)2$ links or paths; thus $N(N-1)2 = 10$ for five stations.

THE CORRECT ANSWER IS: C

FE ELECTRICAL AND COMPUTER SOLUTIONS

84. A router is used to make the connection from one LAN to another LAN or WAN. Computers on the same LAN communicate with each other using a protocol like CSMA/CD and do not make use of a router.

   THE CORRECT ANSWER IS: C

85. In packet-switched networks, discrete data packets are received and stored by the packet switches and then transmitted when a connection to the next point in the network becomes available. Packets are re-ordered at the destination. Only circuit-switched networks require that end-to-end connection is established before transmission. All of the properties except for C and E apply.

   THE CORRECT ANSWERS ARE: A, B, AND D

86. Internet Protocol (IP) operates at the network layer. Both Transmission Control Protocol (TCP) and User Datagram Protocol (UDP) operate at the transport layer.

   THE CORRECT ANSWER IS: C

87. Refer to the Electrical and Computer Engineering section of the *FE Reference Handbook*.

   $1011 = (1 \times 2^3) + (0 \times 2^2) + (1 \times 2^1) + (1 \times 2^0)$
   $= 8 + 0 + 2 + 1$
   $= 11$

   THE CORRECT ANSWER IS: C

88. $\frac{93}{128}$ can be broken into $\frac{64+16+8+4+1}{128}$, which by decimal is 0.1011101.

   THE CORRECT ANSWER IS: B

89. From the K-map, F is satisfied by the third and fourth columns of the first row ($A\bar{C}$) or by the second column ($\bar{A}B$). Therefore, $F = A\bar{C} + \bar{A}B$.

   THE CORRECT ANSWER IS: D

FE ELECTRICAL AND COMPUTER SOLUTIONS

90. All minterms of the K-map can be covered with two groupings as shown below.

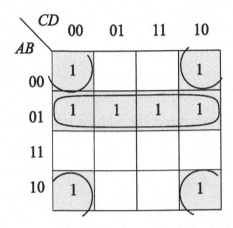

$$f(A,B,C,D) = \overline{A}B + \overline{B}\,\overline{D}$$

THE CORRECT ANSWER IS: D

91. If the count is 10, then the D input to the D-type flip is 0, and the JK inputs to the JK flip-flop are both 1, as shown in the figure. After the next CLK signal is applied, the JK flip-flop will toggle from 1 to 0, and the D-type flip-flop will still have a 0 latched in its output. The count will be 00.

THE CORRECT ANSWER IS: A

92.

Present State	C	B	B
x	1	0	0
Next State	B	B	B
z	1	1	1

THE CORRECT ANSWER IS: D

93. An instruction pipeline performs multiple operations in parallel (e.g., Instruction Fetch, Instruction Decode, Execution), thus increasing the throughput of the microprocessor.

THE CORRECT ANSWER IS: B

FE ELECTRICAL AND COMPUTER SOLUTIONS

94. Indexed addressing uses the contents of some register (R in this problem) as a pointer to the beginning (or end) of a list (array) of values in memory base. An offset D. is added to the value of the base pointer to determine the location of an operand.

THE CORRECT ANSWER IS: C

95. The EPROM will respond whenever CS_4 is asserted, or whenever the address issued by the μp is 100X XXXX = 8000 to 9FFF. (X = don't care)

THE CORRECT ANSWER IS: C

96. The direct address is bits 0 through 8, thus the direct address consists of a total of 9 bits. Therefore the total number of words that can be addressed is 2^9 or 512 words.

THE CORRECT ANSWER IS: B

97.

Step	VAR
1	0
2	2
3	4
4	6

EXIT LOOP

At the conclusion of the routine, VAR = 6.

THE CORRECT ANSWER IS: D

98. $Y = 10 \rightarrow$ loop while is active $\rightarrow Y = 9$
$Y = 9 \rightarrow$ loop while is active $\rightarrow Y = 8$
.
.
.
$Y = 1 \rightarrow$ loop while is active $\rightarrow Y = 0$
$Y = 0 \rightarrow$ loop while NOT active, returns $Y = 0$

THE CORRECT ANSWER IS: B

FE ELECTRICAL AND COMPUTER SOLUTIONS

99. First Round   Second Round
$Q = 1 + 2 = 3$ $Q = 3 + 2 = 5$
$K = 2 \times 3 = 6$ $K = 6 \times 5 = 30$

$3 > 3$ NO! $5 > 3$ YES!

$\therefore Q = 5$

THE CORRECT ANSWER IS: D

100. $K = 2$ gives $A = 17/2 = 8.5$
$K = 3$ gives $A = 8.5/3 = 2.83$
$K = 4$ gives $A = 2.83/4 = 0.71$

THE CORRECT ANSWER IS: A

FE EXAM PREPARATION MATERIAL
PUBLISHED BY NCEES

FE Reference Handbook

FE Practice Exams for all modules:
Chemical
Civil
Electrical and Computer
Environmental
Industrial and Systems
Mechanical
Other Disciplines

For more information about these and other NCEES publications and services,
visit us at www.ncees.org or contact
Client Services at (800) 250-3196.